LXVI®

SIXTY-SIX

DISTINCTIVE

HOMES

PONTE VEDRA BEACH

FLORIDA

CREDITS

SIXTY-SIX DISTINCTIVE HOMES

GDH Architects, PA

38 Valencia Street, Suite 200
Ponte Vedra Beach, FL 32082

www.66DistinctiveHomes.com

GLENN D. HETTINGER, AIA, ICAA

CEO, Author and Managing Editor

DIANE ZWACK

Creative Designer & Production Artist

www.PositiveIdentityDesign.com

CONTRIBUTING PHOTOGRAPHERS

Neil Rashba, Barry Rabinowitz, Joseph Lapeyra, Dan Forer, Josh Gibson, Kathleen McKenzie, Eric Colley, Dominique Vorillon, Wally Sears, Judy Davis, Diane Uhley, Marc Ashton, Paul Johnson, Marc Angelo, Shepherd Boggs, Matthew Richardson, Dan Coley, Joseph Dykeman, Dorian Castor and Antony Rieck.

PRINTED BY: TOPPAN PRINTING CO., CHINA

First Printing: December 2011

10 9 8 7 6 5 4 3 2 1

Produced and published by Glenn D. Hettinger, AIA, ICAA

ISBN: 978-0-615-54160-0

JACKET/COVER DESIGN: The seven homes featured span the diverse spectrum of architectural design that makes Ponte Vedra Beach a one-of-a-kind community, and represents the unique people that make it their home.

LXVI ENDORSEMENT

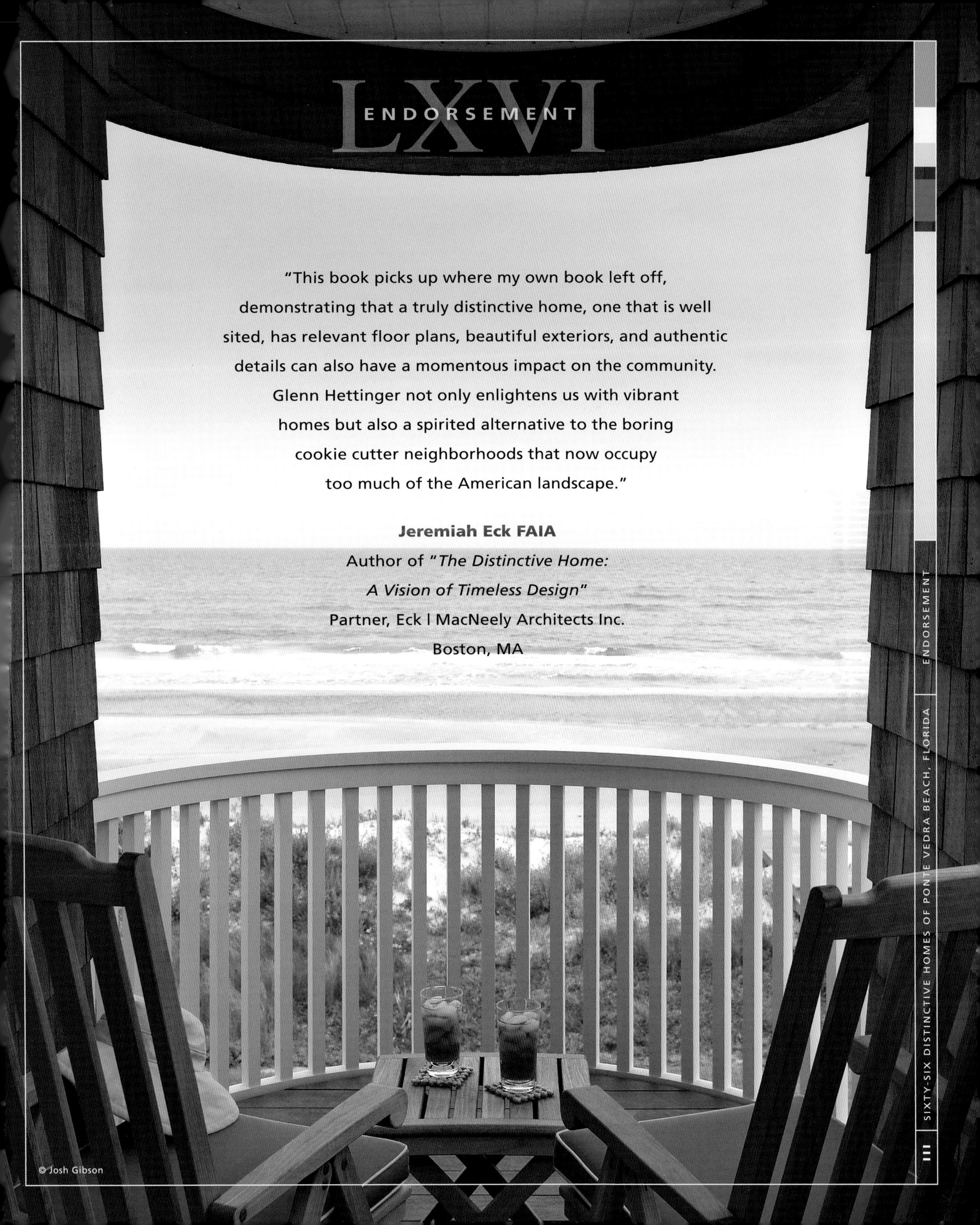

© Josh Gibson

"This book picks up where my own book left off, demonstrating that a truly distinctive home, one that is well sited, has relevant floor plans, beautiful exteriors, and authentic details can also have a momentous impact on the community. Glenn Hettinger not only enlightens us with vibrant homes but also a spirited alternative to the boring cookie cutter neighborhoods that now occupy too much of the American landscape."

Jeremiah Eck FAIA
Author of "*The Distinctive Home: A Vision of Timeless Design*"
Partner, Eck | MacNeely Architects Inc.
Boston, MA

LXVI

ACKNOWLEDGEMENTS

"IF YOU'RE LUCKY ENOUGH TO LIVE AT THE BEACH, YOU'RE LUCKY ENOUGH."

We who live in Ponte Vedra Beach, Florida have been blessed, and I hope that what is shared in this book will be a blessing to all who read it. That's why I have to first thank all of the home owners who so graciously shared their beautiful homes in this way. I had to take these pictures when the sun and clouds were just right and usually on short notice. I do appreciate the cooperation and down-right friendliness that the home owners have granted me.

I appreciate all of the architects, home designers, interior designers, builders, Realtors and other professionals for their distinctive creations. And, I seek their forgiveness for hounding them for quotes, photographs and other information about the homes on which they worked. I hope that all will benefit from this additional exposure of their outstanding work.

Thanks be to the many contributing photographers, amateur and professional. I learned a lot from the pros and the book is so much better due to their contributions. I must especially single out the fabulous photographs from Neil Rashba, Barry Rabinowitz, Joseph Lapeyra, Dan Forer, Josh Gibson, Kathleen McKenzie, Wally Sears, Judy Davis, and Shepherd Boggs.

I most appreciate the tremendous design and layout work of my creative designer & production artist, Diane Zwack. As soon as I discovered her design talents and knowledge of publishing she became indispensible. She is the glue that held it together and made it possible.

I appreciate the many fine friends that I have had the privilege of having as my support in life and especially in this project – author Kevin McCarthy, printer George Ruth, painter Terry Tait, builder David Meyers, the Wise Counsel Group, and The Journey Group.

And most of all, I am so blessed to have the support of my wonderful wife Jean, four fantastic sons Sam, Ben, Greg & Alex, and four fabulous daughters-in-law Laura, Jenny, Heather & Kira. They and my excellent extended family have all tolerated my obsession with taking pictures of architecture wherever I go with them. This book fulfills a major bucket list item for me, but it is dedicated to my loving family as a big thank you for their continued love and support.

Expect The Best,
Glenn

© Barry Rabinowitz

LXVI®

SIXTY-SIX

DISTINCTIVE HOMES

OF PONTE VEDRA BEACH FLORIDA

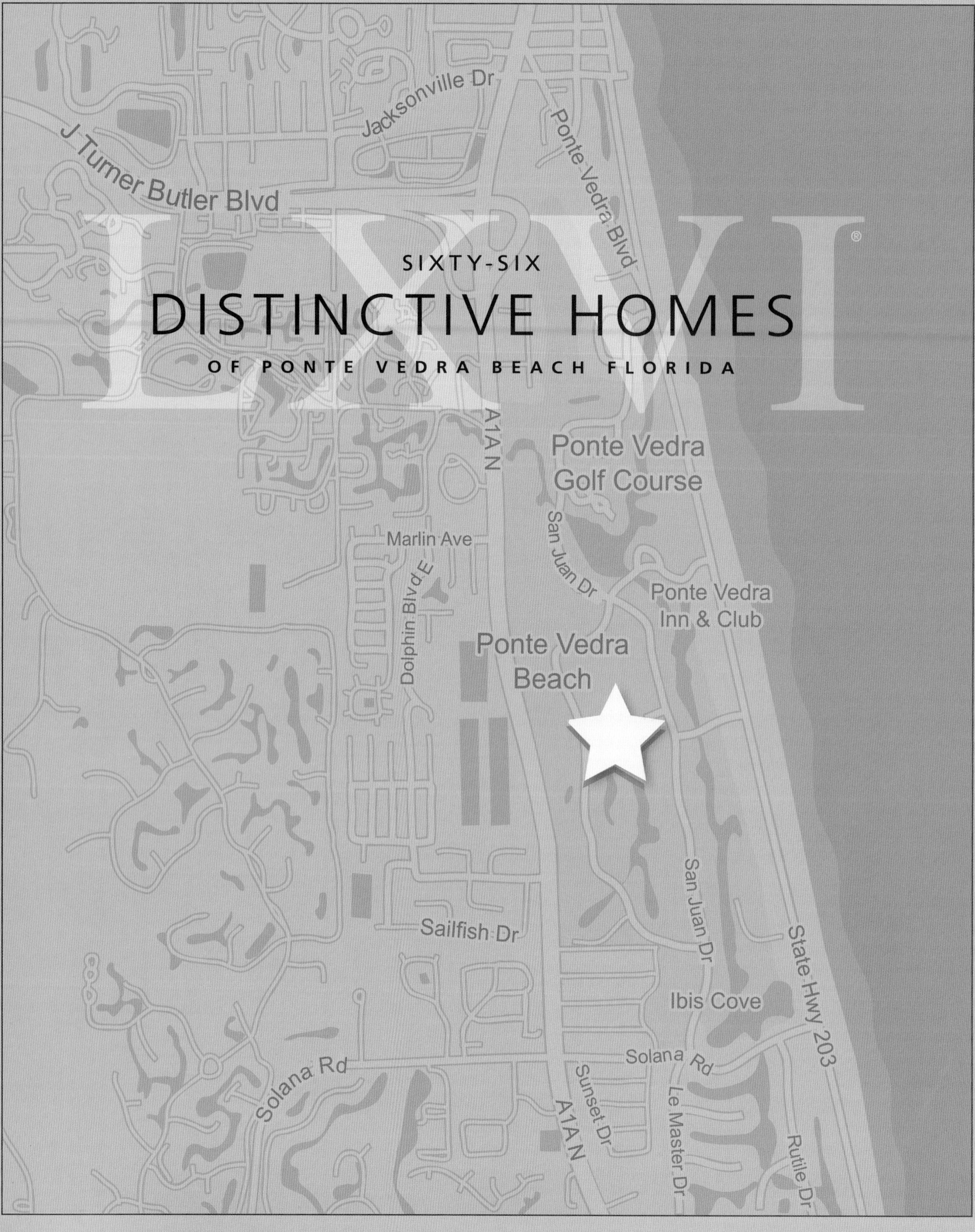

LXVI
SIXTY-SIX DISTINCTIVE HOMES

You might know Ponte Vedra Beach as the home to the PGA Tour headquarters and home to THE PLAYERS Championship, with its famous 17th island green. It was not long ago that it was a mining settlement dubbed Mineral City and a swampy bedroom community of Jacksonville. It is snuggled between the Atlantic Ocean on the east, the Intracoastal Waterway on the west, the city of Jacksonville Beach on the north, and the Guana River State Park on the south. Now 29,000 residents have made it their home.

PONTE VEDRA BEACH
FLORIDA

★★★★★
Ponte Vedra Inn & Club
FIVE DIAMOND WORLD-CLASS RESORT, ANCHORING PONTE VEDRA SINCE 1928
WWW.PONTEVEDRA.COM

MORE ABOUT THIS COMMUNITY

Ponte Vedra Beach (PVB) is part of a long skinny island. The only ways to get there are from Florida A1A running north and south or by Palm Valley Road that runs east and west. Of course you could come by boat on the Intracoastal Waterway or the ocean.

Shaped by a mix of cultures from early Spanish settlers in the 1590's and avid golfers in the 1980's, PVB has a rich and unique history. Haciendas were built in the mid 1500's and the roots for gracious living were planted. In 1916 it was a mining settlement named Mineral City. The National Lead Company built the first 9-hole golf course in PVB for its employees along with a log clubhouse. In 1937 it became the beginnings of the world famous Ponte Vedra Inn & Club. In 1947 the grand golf course designer Robert Trent Jones was commissioned to expand the PVI&C golf course to 27 holes.

Developer James Stockton, Jr. broke ground in 1972 on the 1,100-acre, east of A1A, development known as Sawgrass Country Club. In 1973 brothers Jerome and Paul Fletcher purchased 5,000 acres west of A1A to develop that property. Then they made PGA Commissioner Dean Beaman 'a deal that he could not refuse'. They offered him 400 acres for the sum of one dollar! Not only would the PGA Tour get land for a tournament-quality golf course, but enough land to build their headquarters as well. PVB has benefited greatly ever since from that legendary "One Dollar Deal."

Now the area sports six world-class golf courses. THE PLAYERS Championship annually focuses national and international attention to PVB. It provides great benefits to the local area charities and the general quality of life. PVB is a great vacation resort community and an even better place to raise a family.

CONTENTS

© Barry Rabinowitz

CONTENTS

© Glenn Hettinger

WHAT MAKES A HOME DISTINCTIVE?

GLENN D. HETTINGER, AIA, ICAA

What does Webster's Dictionary say?

DISTINCTIVE: (di-stingk-tiv) adj.

Serving to distinguish or set apart from others.

DISTINCT: (di-stingkt) adj.

1. Distinguishable from all others.
2. Easily perceived; clear.
3. Clearly defined; unquestionable.

What does the author say?

Distinctive is used by the author to indicate homes with unique character, typically designed by an architect as one-of-a-kind. If you invested weeks of driving, walking and boating around Ponte Vedra Beach most of these homes would stand out as being different in a positive way. A few are included more for their uniqueness, but most are award-winning designs, spectacular, and/ or large. Together they provide a plethora of home design ideas and details worth imitating.

How were the 66 Distinctive Homes of Ponte Vedra Beach, Florida chosen?

The number one common thread is that all 66 homes look great and look like they were designed by a talented architect. All 66 homes are tastefully designed with sensitivity to their client's program, site constraints, timing, budget, and attention to proportions and details.

Other considerations included: Were they considered the most beautiful homes? ...the best designed homes? ...the best representative of a certain architectural style? ...the most unique homes? ...or the homes with the most unusual history?

How does the community location play a part in the selection?

Some beautiful communities are dominated by a certain architectural style, site configuration or other influences and are absent of other architectural styles. Ponte Vedra Beach has an attractive mix of Mediterranean, Old Florida, Cottage/Shingle, Key West, and Classic Revival styles with a minimum of Colonial, Arts & Crafts or Contemporary styles. The 66 homes that were selected reflect the predominant architectural styles and mostly level sites that are found there.

Why were some other homes not included?

While Ponte Vedra Beach, FL is rich with hundreds of "distinctive homes", the author chose to limit the books to 66 homes in each book. Some other homes may have been chosen for this book if: 1.) the author had discovered them; 2.) the view angles for quality photographs were more accessible; 3.) the home had been completed and ready to be photographed by July, 2011; or 4.) the home owners had agreed for their home to be included.

Why are there 66 homes in the book?

By one perspective, 66 homes give the reader a lot to look at. But, by another perspective only 66 homes out of thousands of homes in a prestigious community is pretty exclusive company. Besides that, the Bible works well with exactly 66 books. Never mind that the author graduated from high school in 1966.

How were the pictures obtained?

Many pictures were taken by the author from public land. Pictures taken on the home's private property were done with permission from the home owner. Many interior pictures and some exterior pictures were supplied by the home owners or their professional photographer, architect, interior designer, pool designer, general contractor or material supplier.

© Neil Rashba

DISTINCTIVE HOME 1

The Owners - "We wanted our home to look and live like a renovated/ updated beach cottage with the flavor of a John Calvin Stevens coastal residence. Something clean, straightforward and understated. We got just that and we love the size of the spaces, open floor plan and openness to beach views through our large sliding glass doors to our extensive porch."

© Gibson

The Architect - "It was important that it be in scale with the houses of old Ponte Vedra. We wanted the illusion that it had been added onto and evolved over a long time. The brick components make it look like rooms had been added to the original shingle house. The gables and the rooms built into the roof line break down the mass of the house. The iconic round balcony is the defining element on the ocean side. It is like the extended bow of a ship. When you stand on the edge you can see all the way up and down the beach."

DESCRIPTION / RESOURCES

BUILT	2003
TOTAL AREA	5,000 sq. ft. on 2 levels
STYLE	Old Ponte Vedra Shingle Cottage
ARCHITECT	Richard Skinner & Associates, Architects
G.C.	Bill Gellatly - The Gellatly Company
INTERIOR DESIGN	Gabriele Dempsey
LANDSCAPE ARCHITECT	Ben Dinkins Landscape Design
WINDOWS & DOORS	Tischler Und Sohn
RECOGNITION	Florida Architecture - 80th Edition
PHOTOGRAPHY	Josh Gibson, Joseph Lapeyra & Glenn Hettinger, AIA

© Gibson

© Gibson

© Hettinger

© Hettinger

© Gibson

© Hettinger

© Gibson

© Gibson

The Builder - "There is a high level of detailing in every aspect from the structure down to the most minute finish. For a house that's incredibly simple, the details were very complex to work out. The quality components like Tischler Und Sohn windows and doors also sets this house apart. They were engineered to meet or exceed the stringent Dade County Florida building codes."

The Interior Designer - "Because the Owner wanted to use two dining room tables which could be used together or separately, there was a lighting challenge. We couldn't have one chandelier so we designed a grid of hanging lights. The result was a beautiful starlight effect which really sparkles at night."

© Gibson

© Gibson

© Lapeyra

DISTINCTIVE HOME 2

"LAS OLAS"

The Owners - "Some friends of ours told us not to rush the design process. They advised that if we took our time to understand all of the details the architect was drawing that we would be much more pleased with the results. We used that advice and we think that our architect and builder did a great job at meeting all of our expectations."

The Architect – "Our client had the ability to understand the subtle details that define better and best and the desire to strive for the perfect answer to their architectural questions. The whole project was that way. Every detail was reviewed extensively, down to the hand carved Dolphin newel post on the stair. I enjoy working on projects where creativity is first."

"The site was a big challenge. How do you fit a 6,500 sq. ft. home and a three car garage on a 100'x150' lot? The answer came when the Owners asked "how do we entertain when it's a beautiful day outside but the wind is howling on the ocean side of our house and you can't even open up the door?"

HOME DESCRIPTION / RESOURCES

BUILT	2007
TOTAL AREA	6,500 sq. ft. on 2 levels
STYLE	British Colonial
ARCHITECT	Jaycox Reinel Architects - William R. Jaycox, AIA
G.C.	C.F. Knight, Inc. - Lenny W. McAneny
INTERIOR DESIGN	Ward Lariscy, Twila Parrott
LANDSCAPE ARCHITECT	Godard Design Associates, Inc.
STRUCTURAL ENGINEER	Structural Engineering Group, Inc.
WINDOWS & DOORS	Pella
CUSTOM FRONT DOOR	Arte de Peru, Inc. - Gerald Buxbaum
PHOTOGRAPHY	Dan Forer & Glenn Hettinger, AIA

© Forer

© Hettinger

© Forer

© Hettinger

© Forer

© Hettinger

© Forer

© Forer

© Forer

© Hettinger

© Forer

© Forer

"That is how the courtyard on the front of the house became a logical yet creative solution. It actually drove the whole design."

"Why not have all of the major first floor rooms open on to the ocean and on to the courtyard? There could be dinning, outdoor cooking and entertaining on both sides of the house. The courtyard was the perfect solution! I think the Owner's would say, one of the best things about their home is the way they can use both sides on any day and at any given time. They can bring the outdoors into play at every turn, and after all they are at the beach!"

DISTINCTIVE HOME 3

III

The Owners – "We love the open plan design of the interior that contributes toward the beach house feel that the architect intended. The horizontal wood boards on all of the walls in lieu of drywall also lend to the casual cottage feel. We also like that it was built to achieve an AAA rating in energy efficiency."

The Architect – "Our goal was to capture the nature of the Ponte Vedra Beach cottage. We drew from the history and materials of the original seasonal buildings of weathered shingles and painted brick vernacular detailing. Buildings that had a sense of growing over time and being cobbled together as family and friends grew larger. We wanted and achieved a sense of timeless, understated elegance with a coastal feel."

The Landscape Architect – "The use of shellstone pavers for the pool deck, colorful sea-glass tiles in the Key West style pool and indigenous landscaping seamlessly transition the user from the interior architecture to the exterior ocean environment."

DESCRIPTION / RESOURCES

BUILT	2008
TOTAL AREA	4,600 sq. ft. on 2 Levels
STYLE	British West Indies Beach House
ARCHITECT	Joe Cronk, IDAA, Assoc. AIA & Cliff Duch, ICAA, AIA
G.C.	Joe Cronk & Cliff Duch
INTERIOR DESIGNER	Susan Estomin
LANDSCAPE ARCHITECT	Landwise Design - Ladd Roberts
DOORS & WINDOWS	Anderson Windows
ENERGY FEATURES	Rigid wall insulation & spray foam roof insulation
PHOTOGRAPHY	Glenn Hettinger, AIA,

© Hettinger

© Hettinger

© Hettinger

© Hettinger

DISTINCTIVE HOME 4

THE CARUSO HOME

© Dupree

© Hettinger

The Owners – "The construction of our home was distinctive. 113 deep, auger-cast pilings were used for the foundation. To further strengthen the structure of the home, no plywood was used in the walls and floors. Instead, 1x4 v-joint boards were run diagonally in all different directions. Since we've never had a single crack in our 4,000 sq. ft. of marble flooring, it must have worked."

The Architect – "A ring of circular windows invites streams of sun and moonlight into a three story space that marks the heart of the home. As a magnificent dining room, it shares its drama with the rooms that surround it. At the exterior, its enclosure rises up as a cupola that anchors a stately front facade and, at the rear, joins with other masses in a dynamic play of objects that flow into the pool and on towards the ocean."

DESCRIPTION / RESOURCES

BUILT	1985
TOTAL AREA	6,000 sq. ft. on 2 Levels + clearstory
STYLE	Italian Mediterranean
ARCHITECT	James Dupree Architect
CONTRACTOR	David Willis
INTERIOR DESIGN	Larry Lawson
LANDSCAPE ARCHITECT	North Florida Landscape Co. - Robert L. Hartwig, ASLA
POOL DESIGN	Robert L. Hartwig, ASLA
PHOTOGRAPHY	Glenn Hettinger & James Dupree

© Hettinger

© Hettinger

© Hettinger

© Hettinger

DISTINCTIVE HOME 5

"LES CHENES"

The Owners – "The home's exterior and interior, and the furnishings, are designed to capture the informal, comfortable feel of French Country homes. Many of the exterior and interior materials *(e.g. the fountains, driveway, tile floors, etc.)* were imported from Europe. Several of the antique furnishings were also collected in France."

The Architectural Designer – "We were challenged to create an aged French Normandy home, complete with a wood shingle roof, multiple masonry fireplaces, distressed windows and shutters, and well preserved details. The owner is a wine sommelier with visions of a beautiful wine cellar to display his collection. The Owners had an eye for beauty, whether it was art, artifacts, or detailed quilts. With the aid of great team members we were able to complement their exquisite tastes."

The Builder – "The type of construction methods along with products from all over the countryside of France brought joy to me as we were creating this distinctive estate home. I believe when given a chance to use materials from several regions, we start to gain the inspiration needed to fully understand the style and warmth that French Country delivers."

DESCRIPTION / RESOURCES

BUILT	2000
TOTAL AREA	9,000 sq. ft. on 2 Levels
STYLE	French Normandy Country
HOME DESIGNER	Kevin Gray Design Group, Inc. - Kevin Gray, CPBD
G.C.	Victory Homes & Development, Inc. - Victor Yazbec, Ponte Vedra Beach, FL
INTERIOR DESIGN	Owners & Terry Kirkland
DOORS & WINDOWS	Pella Architectural Series
5 FIREPLACES	Isokern masonry by Earthcore
RECOGNITION	National Kitchen Design Award
PHOTOGRAPHY	Glenn Hettinger, AIA

"From the direct positioning under the majestic oaks to the completion this was a fun challenge."

© Hettinger

© Hettinger

© Hettinger

© Hettinger

© Hettinger

© Hettinger

© Hettinger

VI

DISTINCTIVE HOME 6

"CASA PALOMARES"

The Architect – "The owner's wanted their home to reflect the Spanish Revival Architecture made famous by Addison Mizner. Perched on a secluded, high bluff overlooking the Atlantic Ocean was the perfect setting for this Traditional Spanish Mediterranean home. The clients came with a specific vision and our firm was delighted to have the opportunity to achieve their expectations."

The Interior Designer - "In each of our projects we strive for a marriage of styles, the harmony of colors, the drama created by artificial and natural lighting, the use of appropriate furniture, fine art and accessories. When perfectly blended like on this home it creates authenticity, originality and good taste."

The Builder – "This home was a rare opportunity to craft an authentic Spanish Colonial structure incorporating the finest materials from around the world. The mortar set cap and pan barrel tile roof, massive solid Douglas Fir roof timbers, Angelique Teak wood floors, polished nickel plumbing fixtures and handmade ceramic tile from seven different artisans studios only begin to tell the story of what went into making this home an extraordinary project."

DESCRIPTION / RESOURCES

BUILT	1994
TOTAL AREA	10,000 sq. ft. on 2 Levels
STYLE	Spanish Hacienda Revival
ARCHITECT	Hansen Architects, P.C. - Savannah, GA - Paul Hansen
G.C.	Dana B. Kenyon Co. - David Meyers
INTERIOR DESIGN	Vibha Hutchins Design - Vibha Hutchins
LANDSCAPE ARCHITECT	North Florida Landscape - Bob Hartwig
WINDOWS & DOORS	Zeluck, solid heart - Honduran mahogany
CREDITS	Florida Design magazine; Concrete Assoc. 'House of the Year'
PHOTOGRAPHY	Neil Rashba & Glenn Hettinger

© Hettinger

© Rashba

© Rashba

© Hettinger

© Hettinger

© Rashba

© Hettinger

© Hettinger

DISTINCTIVE HOME 7

VII

The Owners – "We wanted our home to be intmate in feel, but deceivingly expansive for family gatherings and entertaining. We also wanted it to feel like the original Ponte Vedra as I remembered it in my childhood."

DESCRIPTION / RESOURCES

BUILT	1936 with 1996 Major Remodel
TOTAL AREA	c 3,000 sq. ft. on 1 Level
STYLE	Old Ponte Vedra Shingle Cottage
ARCHITECT	Renovation: Norman D. Askins, P.C. - Atlanta, GA
CONTRACTOR	N/A
INTERIOR DESIGN	Dee Loop Interiors - Jacksonville, FL
PHOTOGRAPHY	Glenn Hettinger, AIA

The Architect – "This beach house started life as a typical Ponte Vedra mid-century, one story structure: simple but charming ranch type house with a large living room facing the ocean. During the 1980's and 90's these type of houses began falling victim to the wrecking ball, being replaced with large out-of-scale 'mansions' of questionable taste. This is when the Owners asked me to enlarge their house but keep and enhance its inherent charm and scale. To the road side we enlarged the house at both ends, added a modest 'tower' to break up the horizontality and enclosed the L-shaped front plan with a picket fence and rose bower."

© Hettinger

© Hettinger

VIII

DISTINCTIVE HOME 8

"SETTLERS REST"

THE REZETKO HOME

The Owners – "Our low country design is the plantation house in The Plantation. It feels 'casual elegant' just the way we wanted it to. It gave us all of the major living areas on the main level. We especially like the office/ library, family room and eat-in kitchen all relating to the wrap around porch. It affords us outstanding water views. We also love our location within our very friendly neighborhood."

DESCRIPTION / RESOURCES

BUILT	1992
TOTAL AREA	6,375 sq. ft. on 2 Levels
STYLE	Low Country Plantation
HOME DESIGN	CLS Designs, Inc. - Charles L. Smith, FAIBD
G.C.	Benchmark Homes of Ponte Vedra
INTERIOR DESIGN	Ron & Carole Rezetko
PHOTOGRAPHY	Glenn Hettinger, AIA

© Hettinger

© Hettinger

© Hettinger

© Hettinger

Home Designer – "The client's vision was that of the architecture of St. Simons Island, Georgia's Low country plantation style. It was designed from the off-grade brick stem wall foundation to its cedar shake roof system. No detail was left unnoticed or left undone. Each piece of the exterior horizontal cedar siding was pre-coated (painted) at the factory with a process by Olympia Paint Co. This process was the first of its kind, called the Olympic Machine Coat process, and it carried a 20 year guarantee. Even the nails were machine coated and brought to the job."

© Hettigner

© Hettinger

© Hettinger

© Hettinger

© Hettinger

DISTINCTIVE HOME 9

IX

THE FRANK CARTER FAMILY HOME

© Hettinger

The Owners – "Our family's Ponte Vedra Beach home was the fifth home built in PVB. (The old picture shows the very old construction techniques used to build it.) Everything works for our family – a living room with a tray ceiling, beach changing rooms, covered outdoor lanai and arched brick columns. It has always been my favorite home at the beach, and I feel so fortunate to live here."

The Interior Designer – Dan Carithers designed for clients across the world and his designs captured the keen eyes of editors of design magazines such as Veranda and House Beautiful.

In 2003, Carithers was named one of *House Beautiful's* "Giants of Design"— the highest honor bestowed by the magazine; Dan is now retired.

© Hettinger

DESCRIPTION / RESOURCES

BUILT	1929 with 1985 Major Remodel
TOTAL AREA	4,000 sq. ft. on Split Level
STYLE	Old Ponte Vedra Shingle Cottage
ARCHITECT	Renovation: John Zona & James Dupree
INTERIOR DESIGN	Dan Carithers — Atlanta, GA
LANDSCAPE DESIGN	By Owner
PHOTOGRAPHY	Glenn Hettinger, AIA

1929 Construction Photo

The Architect – "The house mixes traditional materials and shapes with authentic charm. Added to over time, its pieces have been fashioned to work together without claiming individual dominance. This allows the casual, low key ambience of an old beach house to survive a touch of modernization and tasteful luxury."

© Hettinger

DISTINCTIVE HOME 10

X

THE DON & MIDGE BARNHORST HOME

© Hettinger

The Owners – "The orientation of the house around the pool incorporates it fully into the living areas. The main living area is designed in an open airy manner to facilitate entertaining as well as everyday living. Separation of children's living space from the adult areas allows everyone his own 'kingdom'. The three story library tower is an unusual feature and it provides a striking element to our front elevation. The library is also an oasis of calm and privacy."

The Architect – "The property widens as one moves farther from the street, so the principal volume of the house is placed well back from the street. Two wings are configured to engage outdoor space: the garage wing with children's bedrooms above frames the fore court and the master bedroom and screen porch wing defines the pool terrace."

DESCRIPTION / RESOURCES

BUILT	1988
TOTAL AREA	5,000 sq. ft. on 2 Levels
STYLE	Classic Contemporary
ARCHITECT	Steven Harris Architects, LLP - New York City, NY
G.C.	John Ingram
INTERIOR DESIGNER	Diane Vogel - Overland Park, KS
LANDSCAPE ARCHITECT	Bruce Ora
POOL DESIGN	SurfSide Pools - Jacksonville Beach, FL
PHOTOGRAPHY	Glenn Hettinger, AIA

"The large frontal gable aligns with the pool terrace, while the cut coral entrance portico is centered on the forecourt. The mass of the library tower balances the front elevation to 're-center' the front door. The plan is configured having a master bedroom and four guest rooms - thought to be a sensible strategy to accommodate adult children with the grandchildren."

© Hettinger

© Hettinger

XI

DISTINCTIVE HOME 11

"MORIAH"

The Owners – "We enjoy the attention to detail, craftsmanship and quality in our home. There are extensive crown molding, faux painting and artistic millwork in the library and throughout. Nowhere is it more evident than with the artistic millwork in the library. The large rooms flow naturally and give an overall feel of spaciousness."

The Architect – "The site dictated some of the distinctiveness of the home. The house fronts a golf course and lagoon in the back. The front elevation stretched to make it one of the longest homes that I have ever seen. It did result in every room having great views of either water or the beautiful golf course."

DESCRIPTION / RESOURCES

BUILT	1992 with 1993 major remodel
TOTAL AREA	13,000 sq. ft. on 2 Levels
STYLE	Classic French
ARCHITECT	PQH Architects - Pepe Perez
G.C.	John Kashou
INTERIOR DESIGN	Jennifer Revson
CABINETS	Amish Made Maple
PHOTOGRAPHY	Glenn Hettinger, AIA

© Hettinger

© Hettinger

DISTINCTIVE HOME 12

XII

The Architect – "The client was drawn to the materials and colors of a clubhouse on Nantucket which became the foundation for the design of this house. Unlike most shingle houses in Ponte Vedra, we used white cedar shingles with a 5" exposure to recall the look of New England. The interior was derived from a study of the renowned architectural firm, Mckim, Mead, and White's turn of the century shingle houses of New England."

The Builder – "This was a dream project for our craftsmen and carpenters – beautiful roof lines and dormers, curving wood stairs, cypress wood ceilings, paneled walls and wood plank flooring."

DESCRIPTION / RESOURCES

BUILT	2007
TOTAL AREA	7,700 sq. ft. on 2 Levels
STYLE	Nantucket Shingle Style
ARCHITECT	Richard Skinner & Assoc. Architects
G.C.	Dana B. Kenyon Construction
INTERIOR DESIGN	Linn Rainey Interiors, Inc.
LANDSCAPE ARCHITECT	Sunscapes Landscaping Design, Inc. Gerry Crouch, FAPLD + Judy Drake, APLD
WINDOWS	Tischler und Sohn solid mahogany
PHOTOGRAPHY	Joseph LaPeyra & Glenn Hettinger, AIA

© Hettinger

© Hettinger

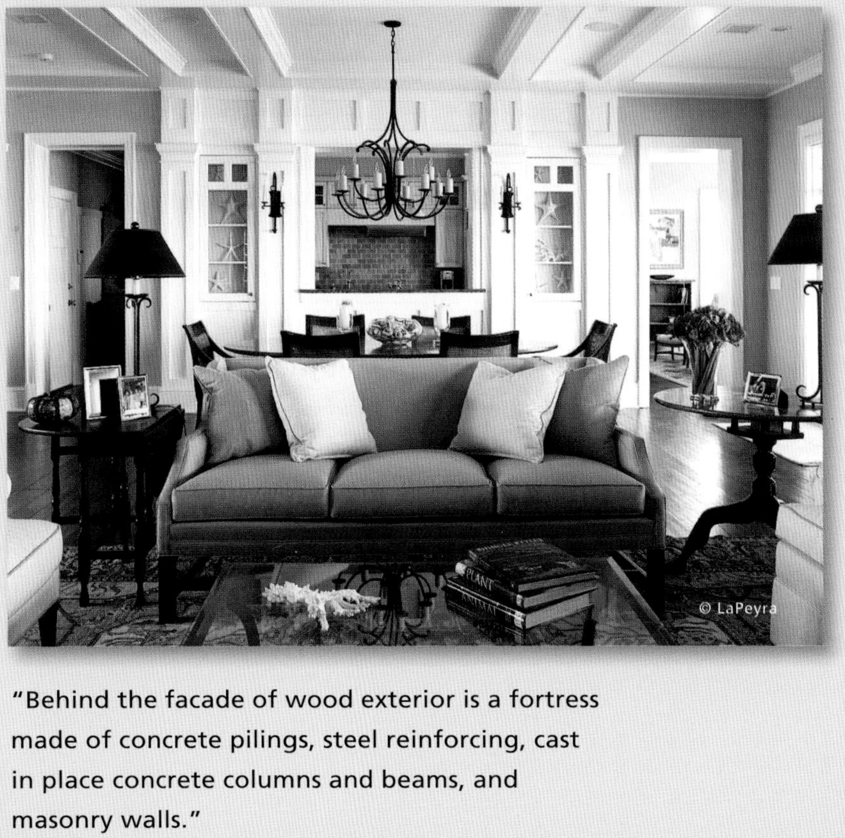

© LaPeyra

"Behind the facade of wood exterior is a fortress made of concrete pilings, steel reinforcing, cast in place concrete columns and beams, and masonry walls."

DISTINCTIVE HOME 13

"SIAMO BENEDETH"
We Are Blessed

THE WARREN HOME

The Owners – "We completed the interior using antiques that we purchased in Northern Italy. So our home is Mediterranean on the exterior and the interior. We love the livability and functionality of our large kitchen and open living space. We also enjoy water views from our porches to the lagoon on one side and the ocean on the other."

Home Designer – "The Owners knew exactly what they wanted and they were very involved in all design decisions. The site dictated some of the distinctiveness of this home. The plans had to be narrowly sandwiched between the lagoon and the golf course. The stretched elevation with its curved balcony overlooking the golf course, makes an imposing statement. The curved sweeping stairway leads to a split-level second floor with game room, workout room, four bedrooms, and a library."

© Hettinger

DESCRIPTION / RESOURCES

BUILT	2002
TOTAL AREA	12,000 sq. ft. on 2 Levels
STYLE	Italian Formal Mediterranean
HOME DESIGN	CLS Designs, Inc. - Charles Smith, FAIBD
G.C.	Brian Lendry Ltd. Custom Homes
INTERIOR DESIGN	Beth Warren assisted by Judy Zapf Interiors
LANDSCAPE DESIGN	Beth Warren with Jodee Evans
POOL DESIGN	Beth Warren, built by Crystal Pools
CUSTOM FRONT DOOR	Arte de Peru, Inc. - Gerald Buxbaum
PHOTOGRAPHY	Glenn Hettinger, AIA

© Hettinger

© Hettinger

© Hettinger

"In addition to the front stair, there is another stair located off the family living area. A two-car garage is attached at the master bedroom side and a detached garage, with quarters above for the older children, is on the opposite side."

Left: Memorabilia from Bobby Bowden's first FSU recruit and first Academic All-American Scott Warren #80.

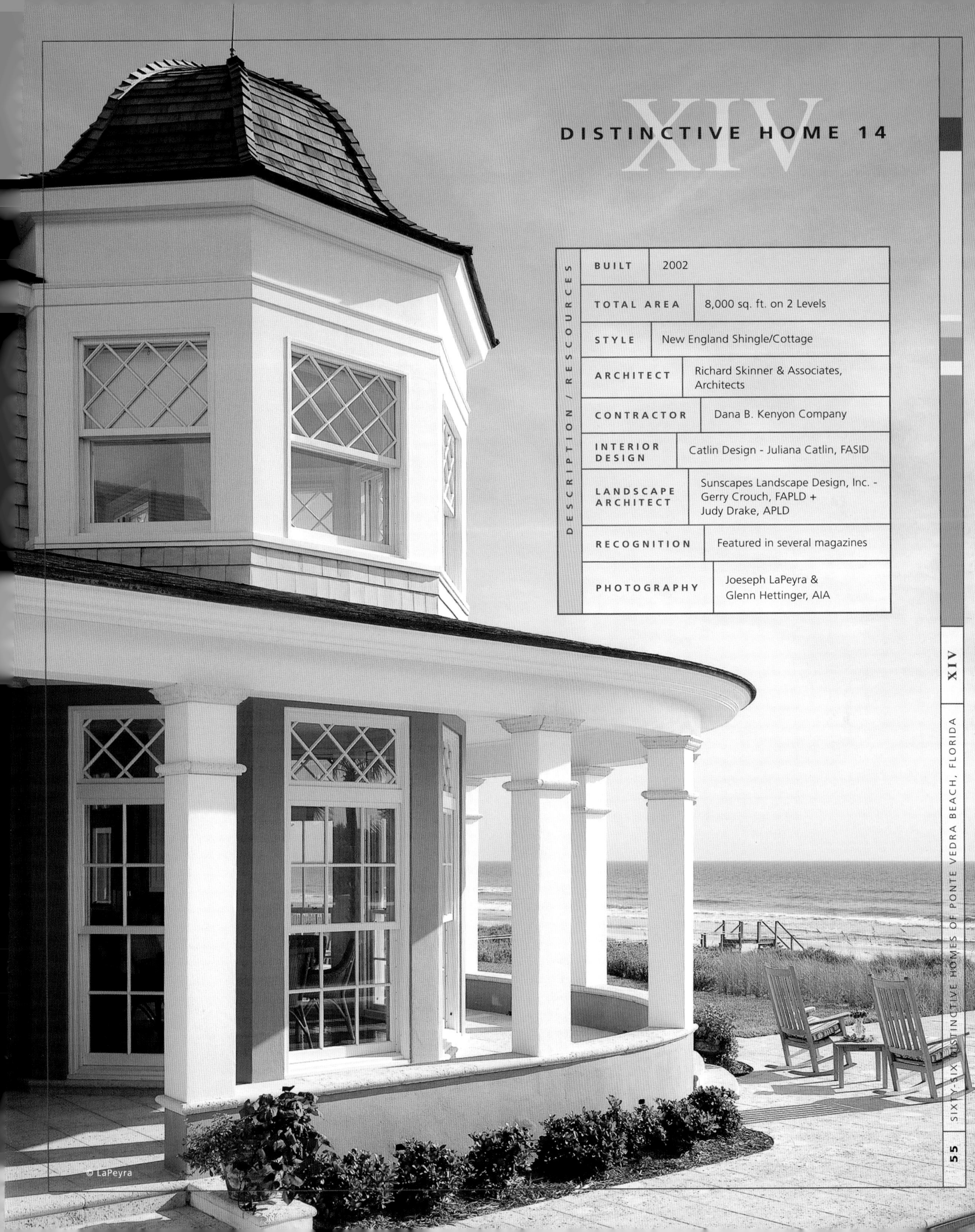

XIV DISTINCTIVE HOME 14

DESCRIPTION / RESCOURCES

BUILT	2002
TOTAL AREA	8,000 sq. ft. on 2 Levels
STYLE	New England Shingle/Cottage
ARCHITECT	Richard Skinner & Associates, Architects
CONTRACTOR	Dana B. Kenyon Company
INTERIOR DESIGN	Catlin Design - Juliana Catlin, FASID
LANDSCAPE ARCHITECT	Sunscapes Landscape Design, Inc. - Gerry Crouch, FAPLD + Judy Drake, APLD
RECOGNITION	Featured in several magazines
PHOTOGRAPHY	Joeseph LaPeyra & Glenn Hettinger, AIA

© LaPeyra

© LaPeyra

© LaPeyra

The Owners - "We just love the gracious design on the inside and the outside. It is so comfortable to live here and the ocean views are wonderful."

The Architect - "The Owners wanted more than a great place to live they also wanted a 'healthy house.' We approached the subject holistically. We designed for quality of space and light, product and material selection to minimize toxic outgassing, wiring designed to reduce electromagnetic radiation, systems designed to reduce energy consumption, and a special focus on keeping the air and water pure. The result is a house that looks great and lives very well."

© LaPeyra

© LaPeyra

© Hettinger

XV DISTINCTIVE HOME 15

The Owners – "We love all of the cozy private areas inside and outside of our home. The front of the home is shaded and almost tropical, while the back is bright and sunny around the pool and dock. It is such a pleasure to have the boat docked right behind the house, and we love our direct views to the Intracoastal Waterway."

DESCRIPTION / RESOURCES

BUILT	1999 with 2009 remodel
TOTAL AREA	6,400 sq. ft. on 2 Levels
STYLE	Country French
HOME DESIGN	John P. Shackelford, Jr.
G.C.	John P. Shackelford, Jr.
INTERIOR DESIGN	Terry Wilson
KITCHEN	Johnson's Wood Working
PHOTOGRAPHY	Dan Colley & Glenn Hettinger, AIA

© Hettigner

© Colley

© Hettinger

© Hettinger

© Hettinger

© Hettinger

DISTINCTIVE HOME 16

XVI

LANCE & PATRICIA CLAYTON RESIDENCE

The Claytons found the perfect site with magnificent views and breezes. To the east is the Atlantic Ocean and to the west is a mile of marshes to frame the sunsets. It took him almost 5 years to complete the work, but Lance designed the Clayton's home in association with an architect and built it himself. With the help of his son Eric Clayton, the Claytons did most of the work themselves.

The most unusual feature of the home is that the structure is all concrete or 100% filled masonry. Thus the shell of the home was completed before any interior walls were placed; because none of them were needed for load bearing. Every room, space and detail was given extensive consideration before being finalized.

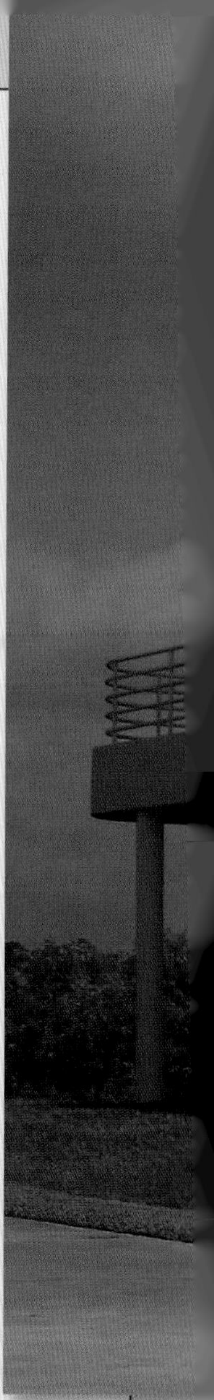

The interior is all bright white except for the floors of black marble with white veining. There is very little molding and it is very simple.

DESCRIPTION / RESOURCES

BUILT	1999
TOTAL AREA	4,890 sq. ft. on 2 Levels
EXT. DECKS	1,940 sq. ft. on 2 Levels
STYLE	Modern - International Style
ARCHITECT	Lance Clayton in association with Charles R. Walker, AIA
G.C.	Lance Clayton
INTERIOR DESIGN	Lance & Patricia Clayton
KITCHEN DESIGN	Lance & Patricia Clayton
PHOTOGRAPHY	Glenn Hettinger, AIA & Lance Clayton

© Hettinger

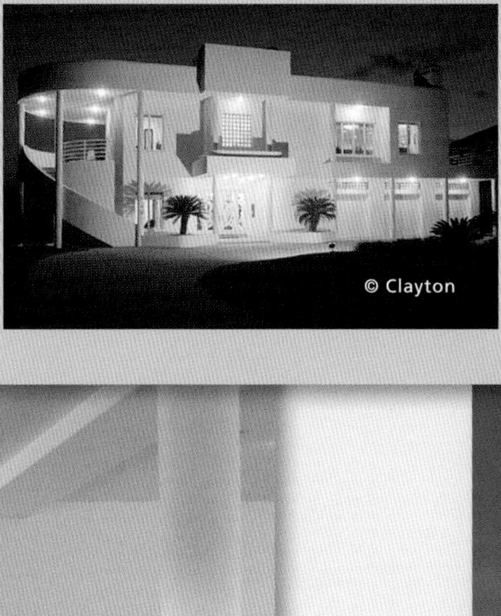

© Clayton

© Hettinger

XVII

DISTINCTIVE HOME 17

THE DAVE & PAM MIDDLETON HOME

The Story – Many of the homes that used to line Roscoe Boulevard parallel to the Intracoastal Waterway used to be tiny cabins of fish camps that served as weekend retreats for their owners. But little by little the fish camps and mobile homes are making way to stately waterfront estates. Most of those estates are built in place, but...

1985 move to Riverside Dock.

Second day, 20-mile voyage to Palm Valley.

What really makes this home 'Distinctive' is its origin and history. This house was originally built in 1907 in Jacksonville's Riverside historic district. Then it got in the way of an expansion of St. Vincent's Hospital. So, Wayne & Kay Stephens paid a dollar for the house, and $40,000 for moving it and making it livable again. House movers trucked the 70-ton house to the dock and then on to a tug-pushed barge. Then they gave it a two-day, 20 mile voyage, during high tides, to its present resting place in Palm Valley. In order to put the house on the lot, only one magnolia tree had to be cut plus several palm trees. All of the other magnolias and oaks were saved.

DESCRIPTION / RESOURCES

BUILT	1907. Moved: 1985
TOTAL AREA	2,222 sq. ft. on 3 Levels
STYLE	Victorian revived to Coastal Cottage
ARCHITECT	Cliff Duch, AIA, ICAA & Joe Cronk, IDAA, Assoc. AIA
G.C.	Joe Cronk
INTERIOR DESIGN	Kay Stephens
LANDSCAPE DESIGN	Kay Stephens
RECOGNITION	*Jacksonville Magazine* June 1995 & 1998 HGTV Special
PHOTOGRAPHY	*new by:* Glenn Hettinger, AIA

Off-loading to new site.

Historic home just after move.

Original home on site.

The Owners – "We moved in in 2002. Anyone living here would have to love the evening sunsets as boaters meander along the Intercoastal Waterway. Very interesting boats and barges parade by on almost a daily basis. Ah, now, that's the Ponte Vedra relaxing lifestyle and we love it."

© Hettinger

Hettinger

DISTINCTIVE HOME 18

XVIII

"ACQUE IGNOTO"

(Italian for Unknown Waters)

The Owners - "We were one of the first residents to replace one of the original homes in 'Old Ponte Vedra.' There was no ocean view from our yard, but when we stood on the roof of the home that we purchased there were great views. Right then we realized that we had to build an 'upside-down house' to capture the magnificent views of the golf course and the ocean beyond. All of our public or entertainment spaces are on the upper floor and our more private spaces are located on the lower floor. We wanted an Italian Country look to the exterior of our home, but we still wanted it to feel like Florida and to be casual inside."

The Builder - "We had a homeowner that wanted a home with a European look. One of our specialties is building a home that, when finished, appears to be several hundred years old, and as if it were in a European countryside. We achieved this by using artisans that specialize in old world finishes."

DESCRIPTION / RESOURCES

BUILT	1999
TOTAL AREA	2 Levels - "Upside Down"
STYLE	Italian Country
ARCHITECT	John P. Shackelford, Jr., PC
G.C.	Curt Howser - Saint Simons Island, GA
INTERIOR DESIGN	Nan Crawford - Winston Salem, NC
POOL DESIGN	Owners with Aqua Pool - Carolyn Sartor
WINDOWS	Marvin & International Custom Doors
PHOTOGRAPHY	Glenn Hettinger, AIA

© Hettinger

© Hettinger

© Hettinger

"We purchased European antiques (front door and courtyard doors) that we incorporated into the home to complement the style we were trying to achieve. We also imported interior doors from Portugal and hand forged hardware from Italy. When combined with our attention to detail, we achieved a truly unique one of a kind home."

© Hettinger

© Hettinger

© Hettinger

XIX

DISTINCTIVE HOME 19

THE FRAN & DAVE O'BRIEN HOME

The Owners – "We never get tired of being here. We love our open floor plan for entertaining and coastal relaxed living. Our windows allow for natural light most everywhere and it nicely highlights the details in the cabinets, moldings, staircase, art, etc. Each room is painted a different color, and the ceilings are a light shade of the respective color. The effect is soothing, and keeps the varied décor and art collection fresh, rather than jarring."

"By using the ICF (insulated concrete forms) we achieved superior thermal and sound insulation in our walls. Our impact resistant windows give us further protection from storms. And our use of low maintenance materials eliminates exterior problems."

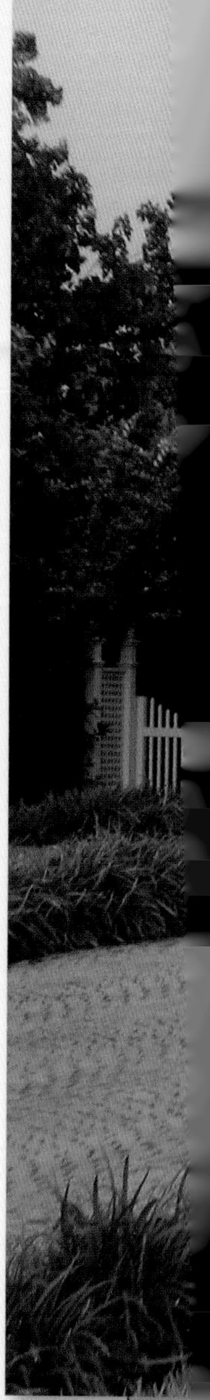

DESCRIPTION / RESOURCES

BUILT	2006
TOTAL AREA	5,700 sq. ft. on 2 Levels
STYLE	James River Colonial
HOME DESIGN	Fran O'Brien with Kevin Gray Design
G.C.	Aurora Custom Homes, Inc. - Michael Lenahen
INTERIOR DESIGN	Fran O'Brien
LANDSCAPE DESIGN	Fran O'Brien
RECOGNITION	*Water's Edge Magazine* - June 2009, & Christ Church Christmas Tour
PHOTOGRAPHY	Glenn Hettinger, AIA

© Hettinger

© Hettinger

© Hettinger

© Hettinger

DISTINCTIVE HOME 20

XX

THE KELLY HOME "EAGLE REACH"

This oceanfront home is one of the oldest in the book and an excellent example of Robert C. Broward's work that spans from 1948 to 1991. Four levels cascade down off of a natural sand dune peak. The plan is designed around a big open central kitchen with surrounding sweeping balconies and decks that include an in-ground pool.

"I told the client that nothing should intrude on this beautiful site, so we will cascade your home down off of the dune so that it will look like it has always been there... and to help define spaces we will wrap each room with wood trim and change the ceiling heights." Bob Broward (7/2010 interview)

Bob grew up in Jacksonville, FL and still lives there. In 1948 he read Architectural Forum magazine about Frank Lloyd Wright and decided to study under Wright, who was 84 at the time. So, he attended Wright's Taliesin West and East in 1949 and 1950, and then received a BS in Engineering from GA Tech in 1951 and a Bachelor of Architecture in 1952.

DESCRIPTION / RESCOURCES

BUILT	1985 - Major Remodel in 2009
TOTAL AREA	6,300 sq. ft. on 3 Levels with 6,000 sq. ft. of oceanfront decking
STYLE	Prairie Style
ARCHITECT	Robert C. Broward, FAIA
G.C.	Eric Pietschker
ENGINEER	Gomer Krause & Assoc.
INTERIOR DESIGN	Jenny Kelly
RECOGNITION	Discovery Channel 2001 Special
PHOTOGRAPHY	Kathleen McKenzie, Eric Colley & Glenn Hettinger, AIA

© Colley

© Colley

© Hettinger

The Present Owner – "My daughter is an architect who worked and studied with Bob Broward. I have consulted her and Bob Broward on all of the updates that we have done to the home. We have always wanted to maintain the integrity of the historical design with lots of openness and a blend with the natural setting."

© Colley

© McKenzie

© McKenzie

© McKenzie

DISTINCTIVE HOME 21

"TIDESIDE"

THE GAIL & PAT COOPER HOME

The Owners – "With a large, light filled, open floor plan, this house had 'great bones' just waiting for a makeover to a cottage style beach home. The design of the entry tower balances and blends the old structure to the new construction. Decorative and distinctive shutters, a signature piece of the owner, were designed with an octopus cutout and then painted a bright hydrangea blue. The front entry porch has another owner's signature - a mosaic entry floor. Shingles, stained to fade out to a driftwood color, were used on the entire exterior, existing and new construction."

DESCRIPTION / RESOURCES

BUILT	1951 with 2003 Major Remodel
TOTAL AREA	3,800 sq. ft. in 2 stories
STYLE	Eclectic Shingle
ARCHITECT	William Leuthold Architect, Inc.
INTERIOR DESIGN	Gail Cooper
G.C.	Dean Russell Custom Homes & Owners
LANDSCAPE DESIGN	Foxy Foliage
KITCHEN DESIGN	Gayle Lewis
CABINETRY	Beaches Woodcrafters
WINDOWS	Marvin Windows
PHOTOGRAPHY	Gail Cooper & Glenn Hettinger, AIA

"A new kitchen with cupola was added with custom built-in cabinetry, to display the home owner's collection of 1950s ball pitchers."

© Hettinger

© Cooper

© Hettinger

© Hettinger

DISTINCTIVE HOME 22

XXII

The Owners – "We have a Shingle Style home with elements of contemporary, traditional and Arts & Crafts design; blended to give balance and proportion as well as appeal. We like the beautiful exterior with its attention to lines and curves. Due to the reinforced poured concrete structure our home is safe and the interior is very quiet. The whole interior is light and airy and designed for a family with children. Each space is separated giving a feel of inviting intimate space."

The Architect – "The challenge in designing this large beach home was to equally satisfy the program requirements, which were many; and still create a warm sense of home. This is achieved through a linear plan, and rooms that are in keeping within the human scale."

"The bell shaped entry is a design driver that is also reflected in the exterior column as well as interior stair rail details. The client wanted a peaceful retreat from their everyday hectic lives. It is both whimsical in detail, and at the same time sophisticated."

© Hettinger

© Hettinger

© Hettigner

DESCRIPTION / RESOURCES

BUILT	2008
TOTAL AREA	8,000 sq. ft. on 2 Levels
STYLE	Shingle Style with Arts & Crafts
ARCHITECT	Mark Macco, AIA, NCARB
G.C.	Collier Classic Homes of Ponte Vedra - Elwood Collier
INTERIOR DESIGN	Alderman Interior Design, Inc. - Erin Alderman
LANDSCAPE DESIGN	Holly Anderson
PHOTOGRAPHY	Glenn Hettinger, AIA

© Hettinger

© Hettinger

© Hettinger

© Hettinger

XXIII

DISTINCTIVE HOME 23

The Architect – "The greatest gift an architect can receive from a client is trust. I was fortunate enough to quickly earn the trust of the sophisticated owners, each of whom has an unusually high level of architectural knowledge. The collaboration was always interesting, challenging, and supportive and the finished project is one of which we are all proud."

"The house borrows stylistically from early coastal Colonial Revival houses of New England while incorporating materials and finishes appropriate to its southern location. The street front presents a very traditional façade while the ocean front opens to magnificent views through broad glazed openings and deep porches more associated with the Shingle style. We wanted to pay homage to the early shingled cottages of Ponte Vedra Beach and hope our contribution to the built environment here quietly evokes the spirit of its place."

DESCRIPTION / RESOURCES

BUILT	2008
TOTAL AREA	7,000 sq. ft. on 2 Levels
STYLE	Colonial Revival
ARCHITECT	A Classical Studio for Residential Architecture - Gregory P. Koester - Norcross, GA
G.C.	The Gellatly Company - Bill Gellatly, Neptune Beach, FL
INTERIOR DESIGNER	Greg Koester & Lori Regner
LANDSCAPE DESIGN	Hughes, Good, O'Leary & Ryan - Atlanta, GA
POOL DESIGN	Aquatic Consultants - Brian Van Bower - Miami, FL
WINDOWS	Fenestra Window & Door, Inc. - Impact
PHOTOGRAPHY	Glenn Hettinger, AIA

© Hettinger

© Hettinger

© Hettinger

© Hettinger

© Hettinger

© Hettinger

© Hettinger

© Hettinger

© Hettinger

© Hettinger

DISTINCTIVE HOME 24

The Architect – "This site has two great views: the front ocean view across the street and the rear golf course view directly behind. By locating the main living level on the second floor, we could take advantage of both views and yet still have some privacy from the public. The landscape design shields the ground floor from the street and the golf course while each room on the upper level was carefully placed to see between the houses on the ocean. I'll never forget climbing up on the roof of the existing house, with the owner, trying to figure out the view. We walked all around the roof until we determined the location of each new room."

The Builder – "As the builder, we had the pleasure of being a part of the design team made up of true professionals working together to create this special home for the owner. The design details were unique and creative and we were proud to have been selected as the builder to showcase our craftsmanship."

DESCRIPTION / RESOURCES

BUILT	2008
TOTAL AREA	7,655 sq. ft. on 2 Levels
STYLE	Shingle Style
ARCHITECT	Jaycox Reinel Architects - William R. Jaycox, AIA
G.C.	C.F. Knight, Inc.
INTERIOR DESIGN	Slifer Designs, Andrea Georgopolis - Edwards, CO
LANDSCAPE ARCHITECT	Ben Dinkins Landscape Design
PHOTOGRAPHY	Dominique Vorillon & Glenn Hettinger, AIA

© Hettinger

© Vorillon

MISTINGUETT
G.K. Benda
© Vorillon

© Hettinger

© Vorillon

© Vorillon

© Hettinger

© Hettinger

© Hettinger

© Hettinger

© Hettinger

DISTINCTIVE HOME 25

XXV

THE GOTTFRIED HOME

The Owners – "We have an unusual lot that is surrounded by water. So, our landscape architect conceived an alternative orientation which our architect accommodated beautifully. Our goal was for the home to be very outside oriented and it is. Views invite the outside into each room which gives a peaceful garden feel inside."

© Hettinger

The Architect – "When you approach the house, you are presented with a building façade that treats the lake in front of it like a natural court or piazza. The façade is anchored by a central pavilion that holds the front door. The approach is completed by driving around the lake, parking in a walled court, and walking down the lakefront arcade to reach the door. The axis that begins with the lake continues through the foyer, living room and loggia, across a screen enclosed pool, and into a spacious backyard and the marsh beyond. A great room with kitchen sits between the pool and the drive court, sharing views across the pool to the marsh while affording ready access from the garage. The house creates indoor and outdoor rooms that enhance and share the beauty of their setting with classical proportions and simple, but elegant detail."

DESCRIPTION / RESOURCES

BUILT	1990 with 2008 Major Remodel
TOTAL AREA	4,300 sq. ft. on 2 Levels
STYLE	Mediterranean
ARCHITECT	James Dupree Architect, P.A. - Neptune Beach, FL
G.C.	Patrick McCarthy
INTERIOR DESIGNER	Kirchner Designs - Carol Kirchner Ponte Vedra Beach, FL
LANDSCAPE ARCHITECT	Ellen Wheeler
RECOGNITION	In PV Cultural Center's 2011 Home Tour
PHOTOGRAPHY	Neil Rashba & Glenn Hettinger

© Hettinger

© Hettinger

© Rashba

© Sears

© Hettinger

XXVI

DISTINCTIVE HOME 26

"CASA SOLANA"

THE RICHARD WILLICH HOME

The Owner – "I purchased the home and vacant lot next door (which sits on one and one-half acres) in 2004. It was important to me that the home backed up to a lagoon that connected to the Intracoastal Waterway and that it had a dock for my 80-foot boat. An added bonus was that the seller was the Jacksonville Jaguar's 1995 first-ever draft pick – offensive tackle Tony Boselli."

The Owner first made many functional renovations like adding an elevator, a new ac system, and replacing the roof with fade-resistant Spanish ceramic tile. He also created a spectacular courtyard to the side with entertaining in mind. After completing infrastructure improvements the Owner turned his fascination with the past into his luxurious present and future. After much historic research he added the interior stone walls, plaster walls with antique finishes and distressed wooden doors and flooring. Wrought iron pieces and antique tapestries abound. And history books can be found in practically every room in the home of this lifelong history buff.

The "Casa Solana" name for the home relates to the Owner's discovery of the rich history of the Solana family – considered to be the oldest family in North America and still prominent in St. Augustine centuries later.

DESCRIPTION / RESOURCES

BUILT	1997 with 2010 Major Renovation
TOTAL AREA	8,000 sq. ft. on 3 Levels
STYLE	Classic Spanish Colonial
HOME DESIGN	Renovation: Owner Richard Willich
G.C.	Benchmark Homes of Ponte Vedra
INTERIOR DESIGN	Renovation: Owner Richard Willich
PUBLICATIONS	*Jacksonville Magazine* 5/2010
PHOTOGRAPHY	Wally Sears, Bradley Stookey & Glenn Hettinger, AIA

XXVII

DISTINCTIVE HOME 27

THE GABRIELSEN HOME

The Owners – "We wanted our home to look like my grandmother's 1934 beach house that had given way to time and termites. We feel that we and our architect accomplished the nostalgic look we desired. We even used cypress paneling retrieved from the old beach cottage for the library's extensive millwork. The arches separating rooms is reminiscent of the original house. The five sets of French doors give the first floor a panoramic ocean view. We wake up every morning and say how lucky we are to be here."

The Architect – "The idea was to use Georgian classical architecture, while keeping in mind the beach environment. We also looked at older cottages and did something that was commensurate with the neighborhood. On the Ocean-side, a wide loggia stretches the length of the homes first floor, while a covered balcony joins the two west-facing bedrooms upstairs."

DESCRIPTION / RESOURCES

BUILT	2002
TOTAL AREA	6,000 sq. ft. on 2 Levels
STYLE	Georgian Coastal Cottage
ARCHITECT	Cliff Duch, ICAA, AIA & Joe Cronk, IDAA Assoc. AIA
G.C.	Joe Cronk
INTERIOR DESIGNER	Carol Covington, Atlanta, GA & Mrs. Howard, Ponte Vedra Beach, FL
LANDSCAPE ARCHITECT	Jim Menge & Ladd Roberts - Landwise Design
CABINETS	Architectural Windows & Cabinets of Jacksonville
RECOGNITION	*Water's Edge Magazine* - Coastal Design Awards, 2004, Vol. 4
PHOTOGRAPHY	Glenn Hettinger, AIA & Anthony Rieck

© Hettinger

© Hettinger

© Hettinger

© Hettinger

"The carriage house garage to the side was given two dormers and was intentionally made to look as if it had been added on, reminiscent to beach homes of an earlier era."

© Rieck

DISTINCTIVE HOME 28

XXVIII

THE ROLLINSON HOME

The Owners – "Our goal was to create a home that fits our everyday life style and allows us to entertain our friends and family with small dinner parties, casual get togethers and large celebrations. We designed a one-story livable floor plan while taking advantage of the views down the lagoon from our back yard. It was important that the house fit into the existing neighborhood, be energy efficient and make use of renewable materials. We feel that with the help of our design team, we accomplished our goals and it is a joy to live and work here."

DESCRIPTION / RESOURCES

BUILT	2010
TOTAL AREA	5,030 sq. ft. on 1 Level
STYLE	French Country & Old Florida
HOME DESIGN	Kevin E. Mullican Designer - Jacksonville, FL
INTERIOR DESIGN	Schulte Design Assoc., Inc. - Julie Schulte, ASID
G.C.	Custom Homes by Bryan Lendry, LTD - Jeffrey Tabb
LANDSCAPE DESIGN	Bradley D. Rollinson
POOL DESIGN	Jane E. Rollinson
KITCHEN DESIGN	CKD, Kitchen Studio 1562 - Kristi Wyndham
PHOTOGRAPHY	Jane Rollinson & Glenn Hettinger, AIA

© Hettinger

© Rollinson

© Rollinson

The Designer - "I believe that each design should reflect the personality and lifestyle of the client. Each home that I design is unique. Listening to the clients and understanding how they will live in the home from day to day is one of the most important aspects to consider as the designer."

XXIX

DISTINCTIVE HOME 29

"HARBOUR ISLAND EUROPEAN ESTATE"

This beautiful home was the 1999 *Symphony Show Home* with numerous designer finishes. It is located on almost two acres bordering on the marsh with its tranquil views. It has access to *Swift Creek*, and the front of the home enjoys a deep setback with a circular drive.

The exterior walls are poured masonry with a stucco finish and it has concrete roof tiles. It has five bedrooms, seven full baths, a home theatre, a separate 1,700 sq. ft. guest house, six-car garage, smart home technology, an elevator, summer kitchen and a magnificent resort-style pool and spa. It also boasts a 1,500 bottle, climate controlled wine cellar. The powder bath even has a 2,000 year old marble sink from the original Roman baths.

© Dykeman

DESCRIPTION / RESOURCES

BUILT	1999 - Addition & Rennovation 2001
TOTAL AREA	9,450 sq. ft.
ARCHITECT	Kevin Gray Design Group, Inc.
BUILDER	Collier Classic Homes - Elwood Collier
HVAC & WATER SYSTEMS	Atlantic Environmental
PHOTOGRAPHY	Dan Colley - Day Shots Joseph Dykeman - Night Shots

© Hettinger

© Dykeman

© Coffey

© Coffey

© Coffey

© Dykeman

DISTINCTIVE HOME 30

XXX

THE JAMES & JANICE PYLE HOME

The Owners – "We love our disappearing sliding glass doors. They open up over 35' wide including two of our corners. It brings the beautiful golf course behind us right into our home. Our open floor plan enables us to view the pool, backyard and golf course from almost anywhere in the house. With the very large open kitchen located in the middle it is a great party house. Our fountain and spa was designed around the spa at Mandalay Bay in Las Vegas. The interior was designed for a beach house setting and around the pool. We have stone and granite throughout the first floor and hardwood up the stairs and the second floor. And the Mediterranean exterior compliments the eclectic style in Ponte Vedra Beach."

© Hettinger

© Hettinger

DESCRIPTION / RESOURCES

BUILT	2006
TOTAL AREA	6,000 sq. ft. on 2 Levels
STYLE	Contemporary Mediterranean
ARCHITECT	Cotner Associates, Inc. - John Cotner, AIA, Fernandina Beach, FL
G.C.	LandSouth Construction, LLC - Jacksonville Beach, FL
INTERIOR DESIGN	Janice Pyle
ENTRY DOOR	Hand Forged by Cantera Doors
WINDOWS & DOORS	Eagle, now Anderson Windows
SLIDING DOORS	Nu-Air
PHOTOGRAPHY	Glenn Hettinger, AIA

© Hettinger

© Hettinger

XXXI

DISTINCTIVE HOME 31

The Owners – "We wanted our home to look as if it was built years ago. Our Architect and Designer worked with us to create a home with wonderful stone and old wood features with a casual feel. Most all of our rooms have stunning views of the pool and the ocean beyond."

The Builder – "This home is full of rich authentic finishes including Florida Cyprus beams made from recovered river wood. Some interior wood doors are from Afghanistan. The Owners were the most savvy clients that I ever had and lots of design ideas came form them. I received a big complement when the building inspector had to ask if this was a new home or an extensive remodel."

DESCRIPTION / RESOURCES

BUILT	2005
TOTAL AREA	6,400 sq. ft. on 2 Levels
STYLE	Italian Mediterranean
ARCHITECT	John P. Shackelford, Jr.
G.C.	Grider Construction, Inc. - Gary Grider
INTERIOR DESIGNER	Nancy Stoddard & Nan Crawford
LANDSCAPE ARCHITECT	Sunscapes Landscape Design, Inc. - Gary Crouch, FAPLD + Judy Drake, APLD
POOL DESIGN	Pools by John Clarkson
CABINETRY	Bennett's Cabinets
PHOTOGRAPHY	Glenn Hettinger, AIA

© Hettinger

© Hettinger

© Hettinger

© Hettinger

© Hettinger

© Hettinger

© Hettinger

© Hettinger

DISTINCTIVE HOME 32

The Owners – "This is our dream home. We live outside, or at least feel that we do, as almost every room opens to and looks upon our pool, courtyard and outdoor fireplace. There is so much privacy afforded by the front, brick wall that there is no need of shudders which can hinder the view. The brick wall not only provides privacy but also offers an element of mystique to the home. People are always asking, 'What is behind that wall?'"

The Home Designer – "The shape of the clients' lot, with homes on all three sides, determined that the home should have a walled-in front court yard for family outdoor living."

© Davis

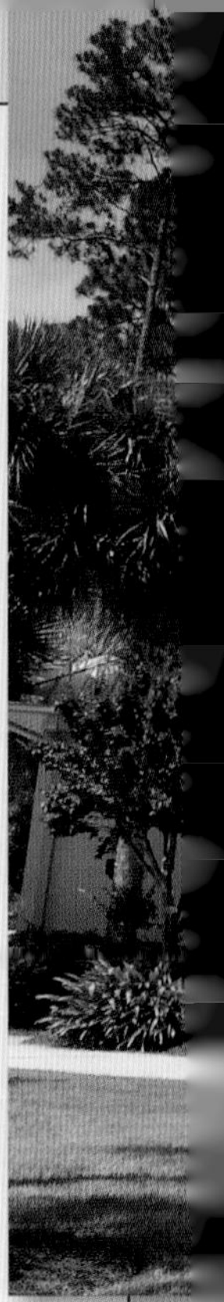

© Davis

"The right side, two-story wing contains the entry foyer, wrap-around porch, stairway, powder room, dining room and master suite on the ground floor. The second floor has 3 bedrooms, 1 office and 2 bathrooms - each with access to the wrap-around balcony. Across the width of the lot is a one-story section containing a wrap-around porch with kitchen/ breakfast, living room, and laundry. Down the left side is a 3-car garage with a stairway to the second floor guest suite and courtyard balcony. The courtyard has a swimming pool, pool bath, outdoor kitchen, and an outdoor fireplace with a trellised seating area."

DESCRIPTION / RESOURCES

BUILT	2004
TOTAL AREA	4,495 sq. ft. on 2 Levels
COURTYARD	1,800 sq. ft. with salt water pool
STYLE	Key West with enclosed Courtyard
HOME DESIGNER	CLS Designs, Inc. - Charles L. Smith
G.C.	Bill Warnock
INTERIOR DESIGN	Lin Rainey Interiors
PHOTOGRAPHY	Judy Davis & Glenn Hettinger

XXXIII

DISTINCTIVE HOME 33

"SERENDIPITY"

MR. & MRS. ROBERT HART RESIDENCE

***"Well building hath three conditions: Commodity, Firmness, and Delight."** — Sir Henry Wotton*

The Hart residence was conceived and designed, with essentially the same three conditions, updated somewhat to the 21st century and applied specifically to the Owners' wants and necessities.

COMMODITY: The use and purpose of the home (its 'commodity') is to be a gathering place for the far flung family and close friends. First and foremost, they wanted their home to be family and guest friendly.

FIRMNESS: The second objective ('firmness') was not just quality construction and a lasting structure. They set out to build a sustainable house that was environmentally friendly in all respects.

DELIGHT: While they were very clear about the purpose and use of the house, and about the way they wanted the house to fit into and affect the environment, they were equally committed to the goal of building a beautiful home and garden designed and executed in classical harmony.

DESCRIPTION / RESOURCES

BUILT	2010
TOTAL AREA	13,500 sq. ft. in 2 stories
HOME DESIGNER	Robert Hart
LANDSCAPE ARCHITECT	Robert Hart with Alec Michaelides of Land Plus Associates
G.C.	Aurora Custom Homes - Michael Lenahen
INTERIOR DESIGN	James Michael Howard
POOL DESIGNER	Pools by John Clarkson
SUMMER KITCHEN DESIGNER	Sandy Ahern
WINDOWS	Luxbaum Impact LowE
RECOGNITION	2011 SEBC Aurora Award
PHOTOGRAPHY	Neil Rashba

© Rashba

SERENDIPITY
© Rashba

© Rashba

© Rashba

© Rashba

SUPER ENERGY EFFICIENT HOME

For more information See pages 210-211

© Rashba

© Rashba

© Hettinger

© Rashba

XXXIV

DISTINCTIVE HOME 34

"VILLA ANTIBES"

The French influence comes from the Owners' love of travel and France. They named their custom home after one of their favorite vacation spots Antibes, which is a seaport city in southern France. The logo that they used for an accent is a duplication of the Hotel Royal logo in Antibes, France.

"We hoped to achieve the French country timeless style that we enjoy in Antibes, but we didn't want anything pretentious."

DESCRIPTION / RESOURCES

BUILT	1994
TOTAL AREA	3,500 sq. ft. on 2 Levels
STYLE	French Country
ARCHITECT	Randy Robinson (Ken's stepbrother in CA)
BUILDER	Castle Builders - Ponte Vedra Beach, FL
INTERIOR DESIGN	John Miller
LANDSCAPE DESIGN	LandDesign & the Owners
PHOTOGRAPHY	Glenn Hettinger, AIA
PUBLISHED	*Water's Edge Magazine* March 1999 Issue

"We needed to achieve great privacy and uniqueness at the rear — overlooking the marsh. Thanks to our design the marsh side with the pool and overlooking balconies has become just as desirable as the ocean side. We even have chairs to watch sunsets that are replicas of the "Boston Legal balcony chairs."

This Mediterranean pastel home with aqua shutters and a red tile roof sits high on its heavily landscaped lot. Yet a small intimate courtyard surrounded by vine covered walls makes the entrance to the home very private.

DISTINCTIVE HOME 35

The Owners – "Major renovations through the years transformed an initial small single level beach home into the two-story home of today. It's dramatic, it's intimate, it is comfortable and the views to the Atlantic Ocean are unmatched. And out our front door we look at the 17th hole of the Ocean Course at PV Inn & Club."

The Architect – "The year 2000 renovation of the house simplified the layout of its spaces, strengthened the axial relationships between them, and emphasized their orientation to the ocean. In part because the building was added to over time, its massing includes a variety of pieces, each with its own function driven character and symmetrical formality. The result combines stately formality with an informal romance fitting to the lifestyle where beach casual can be simultaneously elegant, comfortable, and even playful."

The Interior Designer
"The details of this classic Ocean front Mediterranean home are reminiscent of a seaside villa of times past. Adding elements often found in early Florida homes, we captured the romance of the Spanish influenced style with tile work, a terra cotta roof and cypress wood details."

DESCRIPTION / RESOURCES

BUILT	1970's with Major 2000 Remodel
TOTAL AREA	5,800 sq. ft. in 2 Levels
STYLE	Spanish Mediterranean
ARCHITECT	James Dupree, AIA
G.C.	Owner
INTERIOR DESIGN	Catlin Design - Juliana Catlin, FASID
LANDSCAPE ARCHITECT	Fred Halback
RECOGNITION	*Beautiful Homes of Jacksonville* and *Jacksonville Magazine*
PHOTOGRAPHY	Glenn Hettinger, AIA

XXXVI

DISTINCTIVE HOME 36

© Uhley

The Owners – "We wanted to maximize the incredible ocean views, and while it is a large home, we wanted it to feel cozy as well. A very good flow for entertaining was also important and accomplished. We love the resulting views, his and her studies, elevator, unique sound system and exceptional audio/ video in the media room."

© Uhley

"Unusual features are the 150 year old white pine flooring, 26' hand-hewed beams, cedar ceilings and the sit-up wine bar with storage for 4,000 wine bottles."

© Uhley

© Hettinger

DESCRIPTION / RESOURCES

BUILT	2008
TOTAL AREA	9,800 sq. ft. on 2 Levels
STYLE	Coastal Shingle Cottage
HOME DESIGN	Leon Van Sykes
G.C.	Jimmy Bristow - Jacksonville Beach, FL
INTERIOR DESIGN	Hilary Keefer
RECOGNITION	*Luxury Living* and *Water's Edge Magazines'* and FTU newspaper features
PHOTOGRAPHY	Diane Uhley & Glenn Hettinger, AIA

© Uhley

© Uhley

© Hettinger

© Uhley

© Hettinger

© Uhley

© Uhley

© Uhley

© Uhley

© Hettinger

© Uhley

© Uhley

© Uhley

XXXVII

DISTINCTIVE HOME 37

"THE BEACHCOMBER"

THE CARL & KIM SPADARO HOME

The Owners – "We like that we bought an 'upside down' beach house. The bedrooms were on the lower level and the major living areas on the upper level to maximize ocean views and breezes. In our major remodeling project we wanted to keep a comfortable beachy appearance to the neighborhood because 'it is the beach.'"

DESCRIPTION / RESOURCES

BUILT	1983 and 2006 Major Remodel
TOTAL AREA	5,500 sq. ft. 2 Levels
STYLE	Key West - Polynesian Combo
HOME DESIGN	Carl Spadaro
G.C.	Tom Trout Custom Builders & Remodelers - Jacksonville, FL
INTERIOR DESIGN	Kim Spadaro with Amy Johnson
WINDOWS	Anderson - Vinyl Clad Impact
FIREPLACE	Isokern by Earthcore
PHOTOGRAPHY	Glenn Hettinger, AIA

"We were able to blend the addition into the original structure with wrap-around porches. We did add a new master suite to the upper level so that we could enjoy the ocean views and breezes from there too."

XXXVIII

DISTINCTIVE HOME 38

THE GLENN & DONNA COHEN HOME

The Owners – "The home is beautifully crafted with a generous use of handmade wood designs on the inside. The large rooms feel comfortable yet elegant. Amanda Webster did a fantastic job in helping Donna completely change the interior look with fresh new colors, furniture and lighting. It also has a great pool and outdoor area overlooking the golf course."

Interior Designer – "We were privileged to decorate and furnish this lovely existing home for the Cohen's. They are a long time client of ours and we had completed several other interiors projects for them over the years. The client desired a coastal casual but elegant interior with comfortable furnishings and splashes of color and texture."

© Rabasha

© Rabasha

DESCRIPTION / RESOURCES

BUILT	2007
TOTAL AREA	5,000 sq. ft. on 2 Levels
STYLE	Nantucket - Cape Cod Shingle
HOME DESIGN	Brad & Joye Scott
G.C.	Brad Scott, Builder
INTERIOR DESIGNER	Amanda Webster Design - Jacksonville, FL
LANDSCAPE DESIGNER	Four Seasons Landscape
PHOTOGRAPHY	Neil Rabasha & Glenn Hettinger

© Rabasha

© Hettinger

© Rabasha

© Rabasha

"The clients' existing art collections, along with many new introductions, were influential in every space, tying together the blues, greens and browns of the natural environment."

This New England Country Casual home was designed and built by Brad Scott and his wife Joye.

© Rabasha

© Rabasha

They grew up in Atlanta, and studied and renovated dozens of homes in the Buckhead area. The rustic elegant interior they created here lent itself perfectly to the Cohen's and Amanda's desired design style.

XXXIX

DISTINCTIVE HOME 39

"CASA LAS PALMERAS"

THE MILAM BEACH RESIDENCE

This is the last of Paul Rudolph's famous Florida houses, and it proved to be a pivotal work in the architect's illustrious career. It uses more concrete block and less steel or wood framing, and incorporates large fixed panes of glass. Sculptural form making was always a part of Rudolph's work, but he pumped it up a notch on this house. The iconic beach facade provides the classic image of sculptural extrusions and a less expressive counterpart faces the west road. It certainly hooked the editors of Architectural Record magazine, who published it four times in the 1960s.

The home is essentially a series of seven platforms. According to Rudolph, in this house one locates oneself according to mood. The inglenook offers a nest, the two story portion of the living-dining space provides a goldfish bowl, and the far end of the living area is a cave. Milam has been quoted saying, "It's a great house to live in. Each room has a different mood and you get fantastic views of the ocean."

DESCRIPTION / RESOURCES

BUILT	1962
TOTAL AREA	Over 3,000 sq. ft. on 7 Levels
ARCHITECT	The Late Paul Rudolph
STYLE	1960s Contemporary
RECOGNITION	Architectural Record, Record Houses, 1963
PHOTOGRAPHY	Glenn Hettinger, AIA

© Hettinger

© Hettinger

In the 1970s the owner Arthur Milam had Rudolph add two ancillary structures on either side of the main house -one for a 3-car garage and one for a guest house /studio.

Paul Rudolph was one of the leading architects in America in the 1950s and 60s. His fame spanned the time between the eras of the so-called International School and Postmodernism. His architecture was noteworthy for its unique individual style evident in all his projects.

DISTINCTIVE HOME 40

Possibly the first structure to be erected in Ponte Vedra Beach was on this site. It was the offices for the National Lead Co. to mine phosphate. The office was converted to a home that was in use at this location until it gave way to time and weather.

The Architect – "This new house was inspired by the Mediterranean Revival style with classical European overtures. A relatively narrow depth of building area forced the garages and house to occupy the same facade. The formal front of the house gives way to a more relaxed and expansive interior. Inside, the house is bathed in natural light and captures sweeping views of the ocean from all of the major rooms."

The Builder – "Oceanfront residential construction has evolved into a real hybrid of construction techniques - think bank vault strength, submarine waterproofing and Faberge egg details. Yet we had beautiful coordination between the structural and environmental construction requirements and the finish elements. We had great clients who were completely involved and really fostered a team approach."

DESCRIPTION / RESOURCES

BUILT	2011
STYLE	Italian Mediterranean
ARCHITECT	Richard Skinner & Assoc., Architects
G.C.	Dana B. Kenyon Co., Jacksonville, FL
INTERIOR DESIGN	Peacock Interiors - Kathleen Kenworthy, Atlanta, GA
WINDOWS & DOORS	Tischler und Sohn solid mahogany
FIREPLACES	Isokern by Earthcore
PHOTOGRAPHY	Glenn Hettinger, AIA

DISTINCTIVE HOME 41

XLI

The Owners – "We each had specific goals for the first home we were building together. We worked together with our design and construction team and received invaluable insight that helped us to combine and achieve our goals. While the exterior and landscaping are more formal, we wanted the interior design and decor to create a sense of warmth and casual elegance. We are delighted that each room is comfortable and livable for us, as well as providing inviting spaces for family gatherings and entertaining with friends. Many happy memories are contained within these walls!"

© Hettinger

The Architect – "The site is triangular, with the long side facing the street. The home presents a long formal front, clad in brick, and anchored by a central portico of plastered Tuscan columns. A circular drive approaches the portico and symmetrically feeds a 2-car garage at each end of the home. Between the front columns, the central axis of the house extends through a two story circular foyer with twin flanking stairs into a living room with views through a porch to a garden terrace and golf course beyond."

DESCRIPTION / RESOURCES

BUILT	1989
TOTAL AREA	8,000 sq. ft. 2 Levels
STYLE	Georgian Revival
ARCHITECT	James Dupree Architect
G.C.	Collier Classic Homes of Ponte Vedra
INTERIOR DESIGN	Catlin Design - Juliana Catlin, FASID
LANDSCAPE DESIGN	Ellen Wheeler
PHOTOGRAPHY	Glenn Hettinger, AIA

© Hettinger

"A cross axis offers access to living areas downstairs and bedrooms above. The organization and style of the house are modeled after the Italian villas of Palladio as originally translated in this country by Thomas Jefferson."

© Hettinger

© Hettinger

© Hettinger

© Hettinger

The Interior Designer – "The classic and proportional details of this home make it a timeless design. The homeowners wanted a home for easy entertaining of family and friends that would stand the test of time. The gallery gives the home an easy flow of spaces and is a dominant central feature of the architecture."

XLII

DISTINCTIVE HOME 42

THE HALL HOME

The Owners – "Our design goals included privacy, a Zen like atmosphere and the strategic use of color, sound and light. We also wanted to showcase the piano which is played often. We achieved our goals and have the pool area for an escape as well as an entertainment venue."

The Architect – "The roof pitch, roof overhangs and the fenestration reflect the Prairie School influence, while the stucco and barrel tile roofs reflect the Tuscan influence. At the heart of the U-shaped home are a luxurious pool, spa and patio. The pool stretches the view from the great room clear into the marsh beyond. It has a waterfall and is enjoyed visually, audibly and tactilely while plunged in it. A light system on a timer can even change its color. Moving inside, the coffered ceiling, clearstory windows, custom built-ins, and wall cutouts add visual interest and clean lines. Mark says, 'If the architecture is done well, it should sing.' "

DESCRIPTION / RESOURCES

BUILT	2002
TOTAL AREA	3,800 sq. ft. on 1 Level
STYLE	"Frank Lloyd Wright goes to Tuscany"
ARCHITECT	Mark Macco, AIA, NCARB
G.C.	Brian Lendry Custom Home Builder
INTERIOR DESIGNER	Mark Macco, AIA, NCARB
RECOGNITION	*Jacksonville Luxury Living, Arbus, Water's Edge & Jacksonville Magazines*; Cultural Center of PVB 2011 Home Tour
PHOTOGRAPHY	Marc Ashton

© Ashton

© Ashton

© Ashton

© Ashton

© Hettinger

XLIII

DISTINCTIVE HOME 43

THE PAGDEN HOME

© Hettinger

The Owners – "We wanted a loft-type home in Ponte Vedra, but we couldn't find it anywhere. When we discovered our site we fell in love with the property's live oaks, Spanish moss, marsh views and extraordinary bird life and wild life. Even though the home was outdated we could see the possibilities where we could eventually create the contemporary environment that we wanted."

The Architect & Interior Designers – "Our client wanted to make a total transformation from a stuffy outdated interior to an ultra-contemporary one. We also needed to open up the living spaces to the gorgeous surrounding views. By removing key interior walls and replacing exterior walls with full height windows it allowed the interior spaces to visually connect with the exterior and the solarium. To complete the transformation, the enclosed stair was replaced with an open and airy sculptural stair that led to the totally redesigned master bedroom and bath."

DESCRIPTION / RESOURCES

BUILT	1982 with 2009 major remodel
TOTAL AREA	3,000 sq. ft. on 2 Levels
STYLE	70's Contemporary Revisited
ARCHITECT	Rink Design - Glenn D. Hettinger, AIA, ICAA
G.C.	Dean Russell Custom Homes
INTERIOR DESIGN	Rink Design - Larry Wilson, ASID & Jose Cardenas, ASID
DOORS & WINDOWS	PGT Impact Resistant
PHOTOGRAPHY	Glenn Hettinger, AIA

"A custom, 640-bottle, climate controlled wine storage adjoins the kitchen. We also removed any unnecessary applied detail and trim which allowed the clean pure lines of the environment to emerge. The contrasts between the before and after pictures are impressive."

XLIV
DISTINCTIVE HOME 44

© Hettinger

"STICKS & STONES"

THE TOM & SUSAN SNYDER HOME

The Owners – "This is not the first home that we have designed, in fact it is our fourth. We wanted to encompass something from all of our previous homes into this one – and we did. The results are fun to live with and we will probably never stop adding quirky elements to our creation."

DESCRIPTION / RESOURCES

BUILT	2011
TOTAL AREA	6,940 sq. ft. on 2 Levels
STYLE	Whimsical Coastal Contemporary
HOME DESIGN	Owners with Cote Renard Architecture
INTERIOR DESIGN	Owners
POOL DESIGN	Owner & SurfSide Pools
G.C.	Signature Homes & Development, Inc. - Rex Williams
CABINETS	River City Custom Cabinetry
PHOTOGRAPHY	Glenn Hettinger, AIA

The Author – "This very distinctive home throws caution to the wind and it makes a very exciting abode for the owners. Many home owners hesitate to 'stretch the envelope' because of their concerns about reselling the home someday. Obviously a step into the unusual limits the number of interested future buyers, but it really excites the buyers who share your tastes. Since it only takes one excited buyer to make the eventual sale, go for it and enjoy your custom home exactly the way you want it - without compromises."

© Hettinger

© Hettinger

© Hettinger

© Hettinger

© Hettinger

XLV

DISTINCTIVE HOME 45

"DRAGONFLY DUNE"

Perched on a high undulating dune 29 feet above the Atlantic Ocean, this distinctive home takes full advantage of its panoramic views and private two acre site.

Home Designer – "The home was designed with a low country concept but with a Florida coastal feeling. The Idea was to have a view of the ocean from every room. With the exception of three rooms this was accomplished. Even the second floor two bedrooms and large work and sewing rooms all have ocean views from their own ocean balconies.

"The original home was designed with a side loading 3-car garage on the right front. In 2003 we designed another 3-car garage with game room/media area and guest loft upstairs with another ocean balcony. The new garage has an open ceiling with double car lifts to accommodate the owner's car collection. The added garage on the left side gives it a perfect balance."

© Hettinger

© Hettinger

© Hettinger

DESCRIPTION / RESOURCES

BUILT	1996 and 2003 Addition
TOTAL AREA	10,000 sq. ft. on 2 Levels
STYLE	Low Country & Florida Coastal
HOME DESIGN	CLS Designs, Inc. - Charles Smith, FAIBD
WINDOWS	Pella Windows & French Doors
ROOFING	Monier Clay Tiles
PHOTOGRAPHY	Glenn Hettinger, AIA

© Hettinger

© Hettinger

© Hettinger

© Hettinger

XLVI

DISTINCTIVE HOME 46

THE BURDETTE HOME

The Owners – "Because the property offers beautiful panoramic views of the harbor and Intercoastal Waterway, we used an abundance of windows and French doors. Many of them open into individual outdoor living spaces, each with its own style and ever changing spectacular view. Every room is unique and all are very comfortable so you really want to spend time everywhere - but, our favorite space is the outdoor kitchen. It was with the brilliant help of designer Brad Meyer that the architectural elements came to life. Under his direction we decided to wall the entire kitchen in glass, hang drapes on doorways, chose elegant and yet quirky light fixtures, and completed the house with fabulous furniture and accessories. It's like living in a resort! *Often with many amazed and happy guests!"*

DESCRIPTION / RESOURCES

BUILT	2009
TOTAL AREA	8,000 sq. ft. in 2 stories
STYLE	French Caribbean
ARCHITECT	Cliff Duch, ICAA, AIA
LANDSCAPE ARCHITECT	Landwise Design - Ladd Roberts
INTERIOR DESIGN	B. Meyer Designs - Brad Meyer - Atlanta, GA
WINDOWS	Anderson Windows - Impact
CABINET DESIGN	Bell Custom Cabinetry - Mike Bell - Alphareta, GA
FIREPLACE	Isokearn by Earthcore
POOL DESIGN	Landwise Design - Ladd Roberts
PHOTOGRAPHY	Glenn Hettinger, AIA

© Hettinger

© Hetting

© Hettinger

© Hettinger

© Hettinger

© Hettinger

© Hettinger

© Hettinger

© Hettinger

XLVII DISTINCTIVE HOME 47

THE FRED & SHARON FUNK HOME

The Architect – "Responding to the family's active and ever-changing lifestyle, the Funk Residence was conceived as a series of pavilions surrounding outdoor spaces. Each pavilion operates independently, allowing the home to expand or contract in response to varying functions. Each outdoor space contains activities that express and enrich the family's life."

"Interior and exterior materials are consistent, connecting the living spaces with the beautifully landscaped grounds. Glass walls open completely, further blurring the boundary between inside and outside. The result is a home that adapts for expansive gathering and entertaining while providing a level of intimacy rarely found in homes of this scale."

DESCRIPTION / RESOURCES

BUILT	2004
TOTAL AREA	N/A sq. ft. on 2 Levels
STYLE	Tuscany Contemporary
ARCHITECT	Overland Partners - Rick Archer, FAIA San Antonio, TX
G.C.	Gamel Construction, Inc. - Frank Gamel Neptune Beach, FL
INTERIOR DESIGNER	Karen Orr Interior Design - Jacksonville Beach, Florida
LANDSCAPE DESIGN	Overland Partners - Rick Archer, FAIA - San Antonio, TX
POOL DESIGN	Pools by John Garner
WINDOWS	Anderson Windows
RECOGNITION	*The Atlantic Magazine*
PHOTOGRAPHY	Barry Rabinowitz, Photo-Grafx

© Rabinowitz

© Rabinowitz

The Interior Designer – "What we wanted to create was a feeling of European elegance and simplicity that is timeless and livable. From the moment you walk into the front door you feel as if you have walked into a beautiful painting, and you want to study every incredible detail. The home is full of interest created layer by layer. Sharon has been collecting and working many years to achieve this beauty."

© Rabinowitz

© Rabinowitz

XLVIII
DISTINCTIVE HOME 48

THE SCHUTT HOME

The Owners – "Our home was designed to look like a 'Mizner style' home, but to have all of the modern construction and energy saving features built-in – like low-E impact glass. It was also designed to meet the constraints of our pie-shaped lot. The narrow rear yard has the best views overlooking the golf course. We love our wide hallways, classic stone and wood finishes and a great room that connects to a large covered outdoor living space. It entertains like a 7,000 sq. ft. home but lives day to day with the ease of a 3,000 sq. ft. home."

DESCRIPTION / RESOURCES

BUILT	2007
TOTAL AREA	3,767 sq. ft. on 2 Levels
STYLE	Italian Mediterranean
HOME DESIGN	Kevin Gray Design Group, Inc. - Kevin Gray, CPBD
G.C.	Victory Homes & Development, Inc.
INTERIOR DESIGN	Owners
LANDSCAPE DESIGN	Owners
PHOTOGRAPHY	Glenn Hettinger, AIA

© Hettinger

© Hettinger

© Hettinger

DISTINCTIVE HOME 49

THE LANE & KIMBERLY YOUNG HOME

The Owners – "Our most difficult challenge in this extensive remodeling project was to maximize our space within the rigid permit restrictions. We knew the design influence that we wanted so we gave our home designer a picture book of Moorish architecture. The result was a white stucco façade with pointed arches and Gothic windows. We also challenged the building team inside with the curved wooden stairway that was most difficult to build. With all of our two and three dimensional art inside and outside our home, the Atlantic Ocean is still our ultimate visual stimulus."

DESCRIPTION / RESOURCES

BUILT	1940's major rebuild 2008
TOTAL AREA	4,000 sq. ft. on 2 Levels
STYLE	Modern Moroccan & Turkish
HOME DESIGN	CLS Design, Inc. - Charles Smith, FAIBD
G.C.	Tom Trout Custom Builders & Remodelers
INTERIOR DESIGN	Owner's minimalist approach
RECOGNITION	*Jacksonville Magazine* - August 2010, *Home Magazine* - Fall 2010
PHOTOGRAPHY	Glenn Hettinger, AIA

DISTINCTIVE HOME 50

THE GHILONI HOME

The Owners – "We set out to purchase a unique home that blends classic design, modern construction techniques and many genuine antique fixtures and architectural details. We used Safewall cast-in-place concrete walls. The finished product captures the look and feel of an authentic Old-World home, while offering the latest comforts and conveniences."

"We have incorporated an extensive variety of unique design flourishes, using genuine antique elements in as many areas as possible. The design includes antique doors used as ceiling tray details, imported antique columns, custom metal work and other features."

Benchmark – "A dramatic solid Mexican limestone staircase creates an impressive entryway. The gourmet kitchen has two center islands. One is a custom acid etched marble topped cabinet by Luxor and one a hammered copper topped piece with an integral bar sink custom designed by Bremtown Cabinets. A full complement of Viking appliances blends unobtrusively into the cabinetry. The Norwegian oak hardwood floors and beamed ceilings also add warmth to this hub of family activity."

DESCRIPTION / RESOURCES

BUILT	2007
TOTAL AREA	6,400 sq. ft. on 2 Levels
STYLE	Santa Barbara-style, with Tuscan influences.
ARCHITECT	Cote Renard Architecture
INTERIOR DESIGN	Benchmark Custom Luxury Homes
G.C.	Benchmark Custom Luxury Homes - Rich & Nancy Morrison, Irina Johnson - Jacksonville Beach, FL
LANDSCAPE DESIGN	A.S. Rodriguez and install by All Terrain Landscape & Irrigation
POOL DESIGN	Surfside Pools
WINDOWS	Hurd Impact-Glass Wood Windows
RECOGNITION	*Concrete Homes Magazine* Best in Concrete Living Award 2009; St. Johns Country Parade of Homes 2010 Showcase Home.
PHOTOGRAPHY	Paul Johnson, Benchmark Homes

©Johnson

©Johnson

LI

DISTINCTIVE HOME 51

THE ARNOLD HOME

The Owners – "We just love the beach views, sunset views and entertaining spaces of our new home. We are grateful to all of the professional tradesmen and material suppliers who helped us to create it."

DESCRIPTION / RESOURCES

BUILT	2011
TOTAL AREA	6,000 sq. ft. on 2 Levels
STYLE	Coastal Modern
ARCHITECT	Michelle Balfoort, RA, LEED AP
G.C.	Regional Development, LLC - Charlie Arnold
INTERIOR DESIGN	Michelle Balfoort, RA, LEED AP
INTERIOR FURNISHINGS	Beach Chic Design - Amy Johnson
LANDSCAPE ARCHITECT	Euthenics Studio - Kelly Elmore
POOL DESIGN	Parry Pools, Inc.
SOLID SURFACES	Tile Market of San Marco
COUNTERTOPS	Belmarmi, Inc.
CABINETRY	First Coast Supply
FIREPLACES	Isokern by Earthcore
LIGHTING	Stewart Lighting
PLUMBING FIXTURES	Ferguson Enterprises
HOME AUTOMATION	Habitec Systems
PHOTOGRAPHY	Glenn Hettinger, AIA

LI

© Hettinger

© Hettinger

© Hettinger

© Hettinger

© Hettinger

LII

DISTINCTIVE HOME 52

"MERMALAIR"

THE ANGELO RESIDENCE

The Angelos wanted their home to have a traditional Mediterranean look on the street side and as much Atlantic Ocean view as possible from the inside. With Mr. Angelo's experience as a commercial contractor, initial conversations even considered a more contemporary approach to the oceanfront façade using a commercial window system. To give the house a coherent integrity, the traditional look eventually encircled the house, but the traditional spacing of columns at the rear porches was increased. This minimized visual intrusion into the views of the natural setting on the top of a high sand dune.

Mrs. Angelo liked the idea of a round tower at the front, which naturally became the circular stair. The curve of the tower inspired the use of round arches as openings into the relatively solid front wall. The ocean side became more open with a post and beam composition and the use of porches.

DESCRIPTION / RESOURCES

BUILT	2007
TOTAL AREA	9,200 sq. ft. on 2 Levels
STYLE	Mediterranean
ARCHITECT	James Dupree Architect, PA
LANDSCAPE ARCHITECT	Eric Lycke
CONTRACTOR	The Angelo Group - Marc Angelo
INTERIOR DESIGN	Barga Interiors, Inc. Christine Barga
MPE ENGINEERING	McVeigh & Mangum Engineers
CIVIL ENGINEER	Doug Skiles
POOL DESIGNER	Jimmy Dupree & Florida Bonded Pools
RECOGNITION	Master Pools Guild - 2008 Gold Award
PHOTOGRAPHY	Marc Angelo & Glenn Hettinger

LII

© Angelo

© Angelo

The large covered areas accommodate outdoor living and protect the extensive use of glass from harsh sunlight. As a result the Angelos say, "The grand views are different every hour of the day."

A compass rose is discreetly hidden in the pavers of the circular entry driveway. Then the entry into the house follows the line of an axis that links the mermaid fountain at the front court, the primary formal living area, the expansive "infinity" edged pool, and the ocean beyond. This house celebrates the beauty of its setting and the magic of water in its wild and captive states.

DISTINCTIVE HOME 53

LIII

THE CHAPIN HOME

The Owners – "I have a very nice neighborhood and front street, but I have a great golf course out the back yard. So the front windows are limited and the views are maximized to the back. I wanted our home to have a nice open floor plan, high ceilings and great trim work throughout. My son did all of the finish carpentry trim work and cabinets, so we are naturally very proud of them."

DESCRIPTION / RESOURCES

BUILT	2007
TOTAL AREA	5,000 sq. ft. on 2 Levels
STYLE	Shingle Style
HOME DESIGN	Jamie M. Bryant
G.C.	H. King Chapin
LANDSCAPE DESIGN	Earth Works Garden
PHOTOGRAPHY	Glenn Hettinger, AIA

© Hettinger

© Hettinger

LIV

DISTINCTIVE HOME 54

"GUANA VISTA"

The Owners – "When I say that I live in a log cabin in Ponte Vedra Beach, most everyone knows where I live. Hardly a day goes by without many cars circling the cul-de-sac dying for a peek into 'the gingerbread house'. The rustic interior matches the exterior nicely, making the home very cozy."

"The home was built to house the game warden of the national Guana Preserve. Some people call it Swedish, German, Cape Cod or even Appalachian Mountains style."

"I just know that since I first laid my eyes on it that I knew this would be my home. The location is so peaceful and quiet with great views of the Guana Preserve and its abundant wildlife activity. This is particularly wonderful at dawn and twilight."

DESCRIPTION / RESOURCES

BUILT	1960
TOTAL AREA	2,230 sq. ft. on 2 levels
STYLE	Rustic Log Cabin with Gingerbread
ARCHITECT	N/A
CONTRACTOR	Various Carpenters over the years
INTERIOR DESIGN	Each Owner
PHOTOGRAPHY	Glenn Hettinger, AIA

DISTINCTIVE HOME 55

Note: An added bonus to any owner of this home is that it was originally designed and built for the NFL Jacksonville Jaguar's first ever quarterback – Mark Brunell.

The Architect – "The Brunell house is a very special large, single-family home facing on the ocean. It has elements taken from several styles of 18th and 19th century architecture from several different cultures. In many ways the house was intended to be of the "plantation style" with significant influence from West Indies architecture of the 1790's mixed with the southern planation heritage of Mississippi and Louisiana."

"As the architect, I intended there be a strong resemblance in the Brunell home to the grand estancias of Argentina. This is manifested in the somewhat monumental scale of the house, the arcade across the ground floor, and the introduction of the barrel style terra cotta roof."

DESCRIPTION / RESOURCES

BUILT	2001, with 2011 major remodel
TOTAL AREA	14,000 sq. ft. on 2 Levels
STYLE	West Indies & Southern Plantation Style
ARCHITECT	Barry Fox Associates Architects - Barry Fox, New Orleans, LA
G.C.	Remodel by Morales Group - Ricardo (Rick) Morales, III, Jacksonville, FL
INTERIOR DESIGN	Barga Interiors, Inc. Christine Barga
RECOGNITION	Master Pools Guild - 2008 Gold Award
PHOTOGRAPHY	Glenn Hettinger, AIA

"I feel that the item that makes this home especially unique is the two-story, enclosed, open court space that is the heart of the house and which creates a spectacular space for large party entertaining."

© Hettinger

© Hettinger

© Hettinger

© Hettinger

LVI

DISTINCTIVE HOME 56

THE "TURTLE INN"

This home has been referred to as the "Sea Captain House" and upon examination you can see why. It has a very coastal and nautical feel to it, and it is appointed with many fine details. There is a Venetian glass chandler, a bullnose staircase with custom balusters and a broken pediment over the mantel in the owner's study. There is a fluted arched opening to a dining room with beautiful wall murals and a modern kitchen with reclaimed antique timber ceiling beams. Each fireplace is historically accurate and most bedrooms have vaulted wood ceilings.

© Hettinger

The Architect – "The client family erected the new house on the location of the family's former home on a wide expansive parcel of beachfront property. The house is Anglo-Caribbean in inspiration and has Georgian overtones expressed in its architecture."

© Hettinger

DESCRIPTION / RESOURCES

BUILT	2007
STYLE	Anglo Caribbean with Georgian Overtones
ARCHITECT	William T. Baker & Associates - Atlanta, GA
G.C.	Lenny Boot Construction - Jacksonville, FL
INTERIOR ARCHITECT	James Mitchel Howard - Atlanta, GA
INTERIOR DESIGNER	Phoebe Howard - Atlanta, GA
LANDSCAPE ARCHITECT	Land Plus Associates, Ltd. - Atlanta, GA
WINDOWS & DOORS	Marvin Windows
PHOTOGRAPHY	Glenn Hettinger, AIA & Unknown

© Hettinger

© Hettinger

© Hettinger

© Hettinger

© Hettinger

© Hettinger

"Its slate roof is a rarity for beach houses and gives it a distinctive look that differentiates it from other homes in the resort. The plan orients all the principal rooms to the rear of the home for views of the ocean. Because of this, the loggia serves to connect all the entertainment rooms while providing covered outdoor entertainment space."

© Hettinger

LVII

DISTINCTIVE HOME 57

The Owners – "Our site is a totally bulkheaded point of land that fronts the Intracoastal Waterway and is surrounded by water on three sides. It offers spectacular views, magnificent sunsets and easy access to our boats. The architect's intention was to integrate the outside and the inside so that there was little visual separation. To avoid a bulky screen appendage over the pool, part of the pool actually goes 'inside' and can be screened with the push of a button."

© Boggs

"The open plan flows seamlessly and can accommodate very large groups yet never seem crowded. The spaces are enhanced by the mahogany grand staircase, doors, windows and floors as well as the indirect lighting in all rooms. Other special features include a cabana with full kitchen and fireplace, a separate two bedroom guesthouse, an in-ground trampoline, a 600 gallon salt water aquarium, a home theatre and a pond."

© Boggs

DESCRIPTION / RESOURCES

BUILT	2001
TOTAL AREA	12,500 sq. ft. on 2 Levels
STYLE	Contemporary Arts & Crafts
ARCHITECTS	DesignSpec, Inc. - Werner Hausler, AIA & Lyn McClay, AIA - Chapel Hill, NC
G.C.	Victory Homes & Development, Inc. Victor Yazbec - Ponte Vedra Beach, FL
INTERIOR FURNISHINGS	Lyn McClay, AIA
KITCHEN, LIGHTING & FINISHES	Larry Wilson, IIDA, ASID - Jacksonville,FL
LANDSCAPE ARCHITECT	Prosser Hallock, Inc. - Shawn Bliss, RLA
WINDOWS & DOORS	Zeluck Architectural Windows & Doors
PHOTOGRAPHY	Shepherd Boggs & Glenn Hettinger, AIA

© Hettinger

© Boggs

© Boggs

© Boggs

© Boggs

© Boggs

© Boggs

© Boggs

© Boggs

© Hettinger

© Boggs

DISTINCTIVE HOME 58

The Owners – "It was a challenging design to totally renovate this home while maintaining a good fit for the neighborhood. The second floor rooms and balcony capture magnificent views that would otherwise be obscured by the sand dune."

The Architect – "This plain square summer beach house built in the 1940's was renovated in 1996 to be the quintessential shingle cottage home with room for family and guests. The façade on the street side is casually artful. It gives way to a more engaging wrap around porch that unifies the ocean side of the house. The porch creates a second level of views not available at the first floor because of the accreting dune. At the same time it offers protection to the first floor by creating a wonderful outdoor living space capturing gentle breezes."

House before 1996 remodel.

DESCRIPTION / RESOURCES

BUILT	1940's and remodeled 1996.
TOTAL AREA	4,300 sq. ft. on 2 Levels
STYLE	Ponte Vedra Beach Shingle/Cottage
ARCHITECT	Richard Skinner & Assoc., Architects
G.C.	Grider Builders, Inc. - Gary Grider
INTERIOR DESIGNER	Dee Loop Interiors - Jacksonville, FL
LANDSCAPE ARCHITECT	Sunscapes Landscape Design, Inc. - Judy Drake, APLD
PHOTOGRAPHY	Glenn Hettinger, AIA

© Hettinger

© Hettinger

DISTINCTIVE HOME 59

LIX

This was a major 21st century renovation of a modern ranch style home to make it look like an authentic 20th century Craftsman bungalow. It is on the ocean, and it seems like a throwback in time compared to most of its newer looking neighbors.

The Architect – "We used traditional elements of Arts and Crafts design – grouped windows, wide eves, a sloping roof and dry stack columns on the exterior; on the interior, beamed ceilings, wainscoting and more columns to define living spaces that seem to flow into one another. The richness comes out of the repetition of details and the over simplicity of the house."

© Rashba

© Rashba

The Builder – "The old house had to be structurally reinforced and brought up to new hurricane codes. But the real challenge was in the intricate finish work. The craftsman who did the finish carpentry had never done anything like this on such a large scale. When the home was finished, many of them brought their families over to see the finished product – which really was a work of art."

© Rashba

DESCRIPTION / RESOURCES

BUILT	2001
TOTAL AREA	5,500 sq. ft. on 1 Level Ranch
STYLE	Craftsman Bungalow
ARCHITECT	Lane Group, Inc. - Doug Lane, AIA, ICAA
G.C.	Grider Construction Co., Inc. - Gary Grider, Atlantic Beach, FL
INTERIOR DESIGNER	Catlin Design - Juliana Catlin, FASID
RECOGNITION	*Coastal Castles Magazine* - 2004 Vol. 4, Design Awards - Best Renovation Winner
PHOTOGRAPHY	Neil Rashba

Interior Designer - "We searched high and low for reproduction lighting, tiles, fabrics and wall colors in keeping with the style and to work with the owners' Mission furniture. Floors are cherry, and woodwork, including exposed beams, is maple, finished in a cherry stain."

INSCRIPTION:
...and the sea will grant each man new hope.

DISTINCTIVE HOME 60

LX

THE PATTERSON HOME

The Owners - "We wanted our home to speak 'coastal living, southern hospitality, kid-friendly and party perfect'. Our family and friends come into the front door and kick off their shoes; the kids run straight through the open plan and onto our Intra-coastal Waterway dock. The yard, dock and porches hold much adventure for our grandchildren."

"We bought a 'Florida Cracker' house on a heavily wooded site and we didn't want to lose its character with our major remodel and addition. So we kept the hardwood floors, large open rooms and the 10' high tongue & groove wood ceilings. We were also able to use some of the original doors and windows in decorative ways throughout the house. On the exterior we added cedar shingle walls, a metal roof with matching eyebrows and wrapped around new porches and abundant new windows and French doors. This gave us a flood of light, and a connection with nature while keeping the integrity of the original house."

"By moving the original one-car garage near to the water, we were able to add a large pergola and expanded metal roof that we call the 'garden house.' We use it for entertaining, grilling or just sitting around the fire pit while watching the boats go by."

DESCRIPTION / RESOURCES	
BUILT	1958 — Major Remodel in 1996
TOTAL AREA	3,000 sq. ft. on 1 level
STYLE	Florida Cracker
ARCHITECT	Patrick H. Hargrove
CONTRACTOR	Dean Russel Construction, Inc.
INTERIOR DESIGN	Owner
LANDSCAPE ARCHITECT	Owner
PHOTOGRAPHY	Owner & Glenn Hettinger, AIA

The view, a constantly changing backyard boat show.

HEAVEN SEEMS A LITTLE
CLOSER IN A HOUSE BESIDE
THE WATER

DISTINCTIVE HOME 61

LXI

THE MARK & JETTE WOOD HOME

The Owners – "Our goal was to have a warm and welcoming home for both our family and friends. We wanted it to not only be comfortable but user friendly. Besides the home itself we love the natural setting. Living right on the Guana Reserve we enjoy the abundant wild life of deer, bob cats, alligators and a large array of birds. It is always interesting."

The Architect – "Our client bought their own piece of Florida Marsh: low, thick and swampy. Also, the design of the house had its own interesting challenges: besides the marsh, there was a Great Dane, the owner's hobbies and a screen enclosure around the pool. The 'Shingle Style' of architecture was a perfect choice for their casual life style and to fit into the natural setting."

DESCRIPTION / RESOURCES

BUILT	2007
TOTAL AREA	6,400 sq. ft. on 2 Levels
STYLE	Shingle Style
ARCHITECT	Jaycox Reinel & Associates, Architects
G.C.	The Gellatly Co. - William Gellatly Neptune Beach, FL
INTERIOR DESIGNER	Amanda Webster Design - Jacksonville Beach, FL
FIREPLACE	Isokern by Earthcore
CABINETS	Beaches Woodcraft
POOL DESIGN	Crystal Pools
PHOTOGRAPHY	Glenn Hettinger, AIA

© Hettinger

© Hettinger

© Hettinger

© Hettinger

"The metal roof, the natural brown finished shingle siding and the Ipe wood decks, all helped to create a serene environment among the trees. When you work with someone for two and a half years designing their once in a lifetime home you build long term relationships, and that's the part I like the best."

© Hettinger

© Hettinger

© Hettinger

© Hettinger

© Hettinger

© Hettinger

LXII

DISTINCTIVE HOME 62

"LA NOSTRA CASA VELLA"
THE AUTREY HOME

The Owners – "We wanted the living, dining and master bedrooms to face the water. We wanted open living to flow easily both inside and out. We accomplished family living areas for all ages and several open areas for cooking. The dining room allows space for a round table and easy conversation. The Mediterranean design creates an atmosphere for delightful entertaining."

The Architect – "The placement of the home was extremely important. We had to provide for quality outdoor living in the west facing living area. Our design resulted in a wonderful cabana for cooking and outdoor living terrace, while, providing shade and breeze relief from the summer afternoons."

"The front yard presents a more formal Palladian five part façade, which is consistent with this European / Mediterranean Villa. Select natural stone is used on the portico & corners to accent the quoins. To be true to the materials and stucco application, the stucco has a dry integral color consistent with the craft of old."

DESCRIPTION / RESOURCES

BUILT	2005
TOTAL AREA	5,000 sq. ft. on 2 Levels
STYLE	Mediterranean Villa
ARCHITECT	Joe Cronk, ICAA, Assoc. AIA & Cliff Duch, ICAA, AIA
G.C.	Joe Cronk & Cliff Duch
INTERIOR DESIGN	Shulte Design - Julie Schulte
LANDSCAPE DESIGN	Fantasy Lawn
PHOTOGRAPHY	Glenn Hettinger, AIA

© Hettinger

© Hettinger

© Hettinger

© Hettinger

© Hettinger

DISTINCTIVE HOME 63

LXIII

YAZBEC ESTATE

The Owners – "Charming and grace is what this estate of 'Chateau of the French' exudes. Built with timeless craftsmanship and modern materials this home was designed with sustainability as an integral part. The exterior is an old world plaster finish complimented by the timber breezeway and cypress doors. The roof is a split shakes aged to perfection."

"The interior living and private spaces as well as entertaining and outdoor areas offer the warmth of the French country style. Hand hewed beams and French plaster finish is used on the interior. Flooring consists of antique terracotta and reclaimed oak. No home is complete without a gourmet kitchen which has hand distressed alder wood cabinets with soapstone tops complimented by a French limestone hood above a large Wolf range. The Subzero refrigerators are tucked away behind custom panels. This dream home was built to be enjoyed by many families and through all seasons."

DESCRIPTION / RESOURCES

BUILT	2007
TOTAL AREA	7,800 sq. ft. on 2 levels
STYLE	French Country Estate
HOME DESIGN	Kevin Gray Design Group, Inc. - Kevin Gray, CPBD
G.C.	Victory Homes & Development, Inc. - Victor Yazbec, Ponte Vedra Beach, FL
INTERIOR DESIGN	Victory Homes
LANDSCAPE ARCHITECT	Victory Homes
WINDOWS	Weathershield Lifeguard Impact
POOL DESIGN	Owners & SurfSide Pools
PHOTOGRAPHY	Glenn Hettinger, AIA

© Hettinger

© Hettinger

© Hettinger

© Hettinger

© Hettinger

LXIV

DISTINCTIVE HOME 64

THE MYRON & AMANDA PINCOMB HOME

The Owners – "The distinctive Tuscan design makes you feel like you are in Italy every time you open the door. The home was designed around three massive oak trees and positioned perfectly on the edge of the harbor. It is built on the highest lot in Harbour Island; from the roof top sun deck to the 50' boat dock on the harbor the views are breath taking from every angle. It is a perfect mix between old world Tuscan charm and modern technology."

The Architect – "The Pincomb residence is a contemporary interpretation of gracious traditional homes that have been the hallmark of Florida life for generations. Using materials and detailing reminiscent of Mediterranean style architecture of the region, this home incorporates the kinds of spaces expected for our modern lifestyle without sacrificing the scale, proportion and elegance of its beloved predecessors."

DESCRIPTION / RESOURCES

BUILT	2002 with 2011 major renovation
TOTAL AREA	8,500 sq. ft. on 2 Levels
STYLE	Contemporary Tuscan Villa
ARCHITECT	Overland Partners - Rick Archer, FAIA San Antonio, TX
INTERIOR DESIGN	Amanda Webster & Jimmy Lewis
POOL DESIGN	Overland Partners - Rick Archer, FAIA San Antonio, TX
PHOTOGRAPHY	Glenn Hettinger, AIA

"It utilizes the tight site to create an entry court and to capitalize on views of the adjacent waterway. Heritage trees are preserved and augmented. Inside, craftsmanship - the touch of the human hand - is evidenced throughout the light filled interior."

© Hettinger

© Hettinger

© Hettinger

© Hettinger

© Hettinger

© Hettinger

© Hettinger

DISTINCTIVE HOME 65

LXV

"SEVEN GABLES"

What makes this home distinctive is how well it was positioned on its large one acre corner site. A large portion of the site faces two prominent streets and the house commands positive attention from every angle. In wrapping around the corner the building creates a very private and expansive back yard, complete with a tire swing hanging from a big old oak tree.

DESCRIPTION / RESOURCES

BUILT	2008
TOTAL AREA	6,400 sq. ft. on 2 Levels plus 1,700 sq. ft. 2 Level Guest House
STYLE	English Country Manor
HOME DESIGN	Kevin Gray Design Group, Inc. - Kevin Gray - Jacksonville Beach, FL
G.C.	Gamel Construction Company, Inc.- Frank Gamel, Neptune Beach, FL
PHOTOGRAPHY	Matthew Richardson & Glenn Hettinger, AIA

© Richardson

© Hettinger

The guest home is connected to the main house by a covered walkway. It includes a lower level kitchen and hardwood floor with a full wall of mirrors – making an excellent personal gym or living room. Upstairs is a complete bedroom and bath quest suite.

© Hettinger

© Hettinger

DISTINCTIVE HOME 66

LXVI

THE SCANLON HOME

The Owners – "My wife is from Luxembourg and worked in concert with Benchmark to achieve the European-feel that we were striving for on both the exterior and interior. We have 200 foot of oceanfront and the home appears bigger than it is. That's because our home is one long row of rooms all facing the ocean. But we also used large windows on the opposite side to allow the beautiful afternoon light to flow in."

Benchmark – "We promise our customers that each individual element of the homes we create will be a showcase of creativity, craftsmanship and attention to detail and quality. We think we achieved that promise with the Scanlon residence."

DESCRIPTION / RESOURCES

BUILT	2005
TOTAL AREA	5,700 sq. ft. on 2 Levels
STYLE	French Country
ARCHITECTS	"Bud" Lawrence - Fort Myers, FL
G.C.	Benchmark Custom Luxury Homes - Rich & Nancy Morrison, Irina Johnson
INTERIOR DESIGN	Benchmark Custom Luxury Homes
LANDSCAPE DESIGN	A.S. Rodriguez, and installed by All Terrain Landscape & Irrigation
WINDOWS & DOORS	Anderson Windows - Impact Glass
RECOGNITION	2008 Jacksonville Magazine & Cultural Center of PVB 2012 Home Tour
PHOTOGRAPHY	Wally Sears & Glenn Hettinger, AIA

© Hettinger

© Hettinger

© Hettinger

© Sears

© Sears

© Hettinger

© Hettinger

© Sears

"This was a truly custom project, in which we worked closely with the owners to realize their vision of creating a home with a uniquely European feel on this majestic lot. This home also captures the essence of beachside living, with airy indoor exquisite views of both sunrises and sunsets from the second floor."

THIRTY-NINE MORE

HOMES OF DISTINCTION

There are just too many unique homes from which to choose in Ponte Vedra Beach, FL (with a population of 29,000 people). The author thought that you would enjoy a glimpse of at least 39 more distinctive homes.

© Antony Rieck

© Antony Rieck

GREEN BUILDING INITIATIVES &

ENERGY-EFFICIENT DESIGN

All of the following items and more were implemented by the owner and building team in this classically beautiful home. And almost all of these modern, green aspects are hidden from sight. See pages 108-111. This list makes a great check list for any building team to target when designing their new home.

The home's front view, beautifully conceals its conservation elements.

Three solar PV arrays on each south facing roof.

Owners – *"Our view is that green design is simply one part of good design. We were able to convey in our home that a house doesn't have to have a windmill on the roof or a compost pile in the backyard to be green."* — Mr. & Mrs. Robert Hart

Builder - *"Our desire is to implement an integrated and comprehensive approach to the Green Building philosophy by making a conscious effort to reuse materials, recycle products, conserve water and electricity, improve indoor air and water quality, focus on sustainability and be proactive in energy efficiency."* — Michael Lenahen, Aurora Custom Homes

Insulated Concrete Forms (ICF): Poured concrete walls, using polystyrene building blocks, provide superior insulation value at the exterior wall while reducing the demand for forested wood products. They also provide great acoustical insulation.

Spray Foam Insulation: Applied to the underside of the roof sheathing, expandable spray foam insulation reduces the heat build-up in the attic, reduces the demand on the air conditioning system and electrical usage.

Photovoltaic Solar Cells: Installed on the roof to generate electricity from the sun, these roof-integrated solar panels can provide a significant amount of electricity to power the home's devices, while reducing the demand for electric power from the utility grid.

Insulated, Impact-Resistant, Low "E" Tinted Windows: Provide the necessary air barrier and thermal insulation to reduce the transfer of heat through the exterior wall.

Geo-Thermal Heat Pumps *(ground source water)***:** This water-to-air system draws constant 70 degree well water from the ground into the condensers for heating and cooling the home.

Dual-Speed Air Handlers: Efficiently provide the necessary amount of energy to power up the unit for circulating conditioned air according to the demand on the system at periods of low and high household occupancy temperature differential.

Energy Recovery Ventilators (ERV): Provide a fresh air exchange within the home, thereby improving the quality of the indoor air, while controlling moisture and lowering the relative humidity that can become trapped within the home.

Heat Recovery Units: Re-capture the heat generated by the A/C condensers to supply hot water to the standard tank water heaters, thereby reducing the energy required to otherwise make cold water hot.

Insulating Around Hot Water Pipes: Hot water supply lines within the home, and those located in the attic, are insulated to minimize the loss of heat, while reducing the amount of wasted cool water down the drain.

Low VOC Materials: Use materials with low volatile compounds (VOC) to reduce the emission of harmful pollutants and off-gases which could affect the indoor air quality. This includes the selection of glue, sealants, caulking, paint, wallpaper, particle board, medium density fiberboard, carpeting, etc.

Closed Loop Plumbing System with Re-Circulating Pump: Consolidate several plumbing areas of the home into a "looped" piping system, to reduce the wait for hot water at each device and eliminates the waste of cool water down the drain. Install a control-activated or timer device to begin hot water circulation in advance of use.

Tankless Water Heaters: On-demand tankless water heaters eliminate the need to keep water continuously hot within a tank during non-demand times and saves electricity.

Dual-Flush Toilets: Installing low flow and dual-flush toilets allows the option to use only the right amount of water necessary to flush either liquid or solid waste.

Motion Sensors & Timers: When connected to the bath exhaust fans, they are programmed to automatically turn on during bathing and showering to reduce the amount of humidity trapped in the home.

Sun Tunnels: Used to bring the natural sunlight and moonlight into dark interior areas of the home, these "roof windows" eliminate the need to turn on artificial lighting during daytime hours, thus saving electrical usage.

Energy Star Appliances: Rated for their efficient use of electricity while in operation, many of the appliances available today are approved through the Energy Star program.

Energy Optimization Unit: A device which captures the excess wasted energy used to power-up the home's machinery and electrical devices and stores it to be used in the continuous operation of these same devices. This power protection system protects against power surges and increases the efficiency and life of the home's equipment, while reducing maintenance and energy consumption.

Home Automation Control Systems: Totally programmable monitoring devices include programmable control of the HVAC system, all lighting, exhaust fans, irrigation devices, pool heater, security monitoring and TV and stereo equipment. They are designed to pre-program certain essential energy generating devices to operate only when the home is occupied in peak demand hours, together with timers to regulate the use of non-essential devices during off-demand hours.

Auto Electric Power Charger: Install a separate sub-panel with the capability of charging the electric powered automobiles. These vehicles will lessen the dependency on foreign fuels, as well as the emission of carbon dioxide into the atmosphere.

Recycled Materials: Recycled materials lessen the impact on our natural resources. Synthetic gypsum (calcium sulfate) used for sheetrock is actually a by-product of the desulfurization process that coal-fired power plants use to reduce air pollution.

Reclaimed Materials: Reclaimed lumber lessens the need to harvest new forest growth. Wood beams (pine and oak) are reclaimed from older wooden structures and are being reused in their natural state to create a worn, authentic look. Cedar beams have been reclaimed from underwater marshy bogs and given new life as structural timbers.

Low Maintenance Materials: The use of synthetic exterior building materials, such as trim boards manufactured from PVC products, offer a long term solution to low maintenance by eliminating any cracking, rotting, splitting or moisture penetration. Synthetic decking materials made from recycled wood fiber, sawdust and plastic scrap provide a durable, moisture resistant alternative to wood deck products.

Collection of Rain Water: A 20,000 gallon underground cistern will capture all of the rain water from the roof in a holding tank for use as the primary source of irrigation for the lawn and plantings.

Pervious Surfaces for the Driveway and Patios: Decorative concrete pavers and sand-set stone are used, in lieu of poured concrete, to allow percolation of water into the ground, reducing the water run-off into the storm drainage system and waterways.

Geothermal heat pumps.

Sand-set pavers allow water to percolate into the storm drainage system and waterways.

Native Plants: The selection of native Florida trees and plants, which require less watering in this hot summer / mild winter climate, will reduce the demand on irrigation usage.

Bio-swale: Incorporated into the landscape design, and adjacent to the natural waterway, this bio-swale with river rock and drought-tolerant plantings is intended to capture the flow of surface water, thereby reducing the run-off of fertilizer and contaminated water into the storm drainage system and lagoon.

TWENTY-SEVEN MORE
DISTINCTIVE ENTRYWAYS

In addition to the 66 distinctive homes featured, please enjoy 27 more distinctive entryways of other Ponte Vedra Beach homes.

PONTE VEDRA BEACH

CHAMBER OF COMMERCE

If you would like to know more about what it would be like to live and/ or work in the Ponte Vedra Beach community, please check us out at HYPERLINK "http://www.pontevedrachamber.org."

Ponte Vedra Beach is an unincorporated seaside community in St. Johns County, Florida. It is located 18 miles southeast of Jacksonville and 26 miles north of America's oldest city St. Augustine. It is an upscale tourist resort best known for its professional caliber golf, world class tennis and pristine beaches.

Photography by Alex Quijano

We are home to the ATP Tour, the PGA Tour and THE PLAYERS Championship, which is considered the "fifth" major golf tournament in the world. Several years ago, it was voted the best place to live in Florida by *Money Magazine*.

You will find the ambiance of a small town here, but with the flavor of sophistication found in larger cities. Wonderful housing options, excellent schools, world-class healthcare, gourmet dining, a new concert hall and a thriving cultural center enhance the living experience in Ponte Vedra Beach.

PONTE VEDRA BEACH
Chamber of Commerce

The Cultural Center's

mission

is to bring the arts into the life of our community.

The Cultural Center at Ponte Vedra Beach
operates artist galleries and studios and provides
arts education programs reaching more than 8,000 supporters,
members and participants annually.
Programs include exhibitions of locally and nationally known
artists, art classes and workshops for children and adults, children's
arts camps and arts outreach programs serving children
with special needs within our community.
The Cultural Center at Ponte Vedra Beach also produces major
fundraising events each year including

"The Ponte Vedra Beach Home and Art Tour."

The Cultural Center
AT PONTE VEDRA BEACH

www.ccpvb.org

The Cultural Center at Ponte Vedra Beach is a 501(c)3 non-profit organization.
Proceeds raised from events directly benefit our arts education programs.

DISTINCTIVE GUIDE

Discover more information on these resources by visiting www.66DistinctiveHomes.com.

ARCHITECTS & DESIGNERS

Richard Skinner & Associates, Architects
Richard G. Skinner III, AIA, LEED AP
Jacksonville, FL
D.Homes: #1, #12, #14, #40, #58

Jaycox Reinel Architects
William R. Jaycox, AIA
Jacksonville, FL
D.Homes: #2, #24, #61

Cliff Duch, ICAA, AIA
& Joe Cronk, ICAA
Jacksonville, FL
D.Homes: #3, #17, #27, #62

James Dupree Architect
Jacksonville Beach, FL
D.Homes: #4, #9, #25, #35, #41, #52

Overland Partners
Rick Archer, FAIA
San Antonio, TX
D.Homes: #47, #64

Hansen Architects, P.C.
Paul Hansen
Savannah, GA
D. Home: #6

Steven Harris Architects, LLP
New York City, NY
D. Home: #10

PQH Architects Group - Pepe Perez
Jacksonville, FL
D. Home: #11

John P. Shackelford, Jr., PC
D. Homes: #15, #18, #31

Robert C. Brown, FAIA
Jacksonville, FL
D. Home: #20

Cote Renard Architecture
Jacksonville, FL
D. Home #44, #50

William Leuthold Architect, Inc.
Jacksonville, FL
D. Home: #21

Cliff Duch, ICAA, AIA
Jacksonville, FL
D. Home: #46

Mark Macco, AIA, NCARB
Ponte Vedra Beach, FL
D. Homes: #22, #42

Gregory P. Koester, AIA
New York City, NY
D. Home: #23

Cotner Associates, Inc.
John Cotner, AIA
Fernandina Beach, FL
D. Home: #30

The Late Paul Rudolph 1963 Architectural Record Home
Jacksonville, FL
D. Home: #39

Barry Fox Associates Architects – Barry Fox
New Orleans, LA
D. Home: #55

William T. Baker & Associates
Atlanta, GA
D. Home: #56

Glenn Hettinger, AIA, ICAA
Ponte Vedra Beach, FL
D. Home: #43

Michelle Balfoort, RA, LEED AP
Miami, FL – D. Home: #51

DesignSpec, Inc.
Werner Hausler, AIA
& Lyn McClay, AIA
Chapel Hill, NC
D. Home: #57

Lane Group, Inc.
Doug Lane, AIA, ICAA
Jacksonville, FL
D. Home: #59

Patrick H. Hargrove
D. Home: #60

Bud Lawrence
Ft. Myers, FL
D. Home: #66

HOME DESIGNERS

Kevin Gray Design Group, Inc.
Kevin Gray, CPBD
D. Homes: #5, #19, #29, #48, #63, #65

CLS Designs, Inc.
Charles L. Smith, FAIBD
D. Homes: #8, #13, #31, #45, #49

Kevin E. Mullican
D. Home: #28

Brad & Joye Scott
D. Home: #38

Robert Hart
D. Home: #33

Jamie M. Bryant
D. Home: #53

Leon Van Sykes
D. Home: #36

INTERIOR DESIGN & DECORATING

Catlin Design
Juliana Catlin, FASID
Jacksonville, FL
D. Homes: #12, #35, #41, #59

Amanda Webster Design
Amanda Webster, ASID
Jacksonville Beach, FL
D. Homes: #38, #61, #64

Dee Loop Interiors
Jacksonville, FL
D. Homes: #7, #58

Gabriele Dempsey
D. Home: #1

Ward Lariscy & Twila Parrott
D. Home: #2

Susan Estomin
D. Home: #1

Kirchner Designs
Carol Kirchner
Ponte Vedra Beach, FL
D. Home: #25

Vibha Hutchins Design
Vibha Hutchins
Jacksonville, FL
D. Home: #6

Linn Rainey Interiors, Inc.
D. Homes: #12, #31

Judy Zapf Interiors
D. Home: #13

Alderman Interior Design, Inc.
Erin Alderman
D. Home: #22

Nan Crawford
Winston Salem, NC
D. Homes: #18, #31

Gail Cooper
Ponte Vedra Beach, FL
D. Home: #21

Slifer Designs
Andrea Georgopolis
Edwards, CO
D. Home: #24

Terry Kirkland
D. Home: #6

Peacock Interiors
Kathleen Kenworthy
Atlanta, GA
D. Home: #40

Carol Covington
Atlanta, GA
D. Home: #27

Mrs. Howard
Ponte Vedra Beach, FL
D. Home: #27

Phoebe Howard
Atlanta, GA
D. Home: #56

Schulte Design Assoc., Inc.
Julie Schulte, ASID
Ponte Vedra Beach, FL
D. Homes: #28, #62

James Michael Howard Interiors
James Howard
Jacksonville, FL
D. Home: #33;
Atlanta, GA - #56

Barga Interiors, Inc.
Christine Barga
D. Homes: #52 #55

Benchmark Custom Luxury Homes
Jacksonville Beach, FL
D. Homes: #50, #66

Larry Wilson, ASID
Jacksonville, FL
D. Homes: #43, #57

Jose Cardenas, ASID
Jacksonville, FL
D. Home: #43

Mark Macco, AIA, NCARB
Ponte Vedra Beach, FL
D. Home: #42

B. Meyer Designs
Brad Meyer
Atlanta, GA
D. Home: #46

Karen Orr Interior Design
Jacksonville Beach, FL
D. Home: #47

Michelle Balfoort, RA, LEED AP
Miami, FL
D. Home: #51

Hilary Keefer
D. Home: #36

Amy Johnson
D. Home: #37

Tom & Susan Snyder
Ponte Vedra Beach, FL
D. Home: #44

LANDSCAPE DESIGN

Sunscapes Landscape Design, Inc.
Gerry Crouch, FAPLD &
Judy Drake, APLD
Jacksonville, FL
D. Homes: #12, #14, #31, #58

Landwise Design
Ladd Roberts
Jacksonville, FL
D. Homes: #3, #27, #46

Overland Partners
Rick Archer, FAIA
San Antonio, TX
D.Homes: #47, #64

North Florida Landscape Co.
Robert L. Hartwig, ASLA
D. Homes: #4, #6

A.S. Rodriguez
D. Homes: #50, #66

Godard Design Associates, Inc.
D. Home: #2

Foxy Foliage - D. Home: #21

Holly Anderson - D. Home: #22

Hughes, Good, O'Leary & Ryan
Atlanta, GA – D. Home: #23

Ellen Wheeler
D. Homes: #25, #41

Land Plus Associates
Alec Michaelides
Atlanta, GA
D. Home: #33, #56

Prosser Hallock, Inc.
Shawn Bliss
Jacksonville, FL
D. Home: #57

Ben Jenkins Landscape Design
D. Home: #24

Fred Halback - D. Home: #35

Four Seasons Landscape
D. Home: #38

Ben Dinkins Landscape Design
D. Home: #1

Euthenics Studio
Kelly Elmore
D. Home: #51

Eric Lycke
D. Home: #52

Earth Works Garden
D. Home: #53

GENERAL CONTRACTORS

Victory Homes & Development, Inc.
Victor Yazbec
Ponte Vedra Beach, FL
D. Homes: #5, #48, #57, #63

Grider Construction, Inc.
Gary Grider
Atlantic Beach, FL
D. Homes: #31, #58, #59

The Gellatly Company
William Gellatly
Neptune Beach, FL
D. Homes: #1, #23, #61

Dana B. Kenyon Company
Jacksonville, FL
D. Homes: #6, #12, #40

Dean Russell Custom Homes
Dean Russell
Jacksonville Beach, FL
D. Homes: #21, #43, #60

Custom Homes by Bryan Lendry, LTD.
Jeffrey Tabb
D. Homes: #12, #28, #42

Aurora Custom Homes, Inc.
Michael Lenahen
Ponte Vedra Beach, FL
D. Homes: #19, #33

Benchmark Homes of Ponte Vedra
Ponte Vedra Beach, FL
D. Homes: #17, #26

Collier Classic Homes of Ponte Vedra
Elwood Collier
Ponte Vedra Beach, FL
D. Homes: #22, #29, #41

Benchmark Custom Luxury Homes
Jacksonville Beach, FL
D. Homes: #50, #66

Tom Trout Custom Builders & Remodelers
Jacksonville, FL
D. Homes: #37, #49

Gamel Construction Company, Inc.
Frank Gamel
Neptune Beach, FL
D. Homes: #47, #65

C.F. Knight, Inc.
Lenny McAneny & Finley Knight
Jacksonville, FL
D. Homes: #2, #24

LandSouth Construction, LLC.
James Pyle
Jacksonville Beach, FL
D. Home: #30

Brad Scott
Ponte Vedra Beach, FL
D. Home: #38

Signature Homes & Development, Inc.
Rex Williams
Jacksonville, FL
D. Home: #44

Morales Group
Ricardo Morales, III
Jacksonville, FL
D. Home: #55

Regional Development, LLC
Charlie Arnold
Ponte Vedra Beach, FL
D. Home: #51

The Angelo Group
Marc Angelo
Ponte Vedra Beach, FL
D. Home: #52

Lenny Boot Construction
Jacksonville, FL
D. Home: #56

Castle Builders
Paul Cooney
Ponte Vedra Beach, FL
D. Home: #34

Jimmy Bristow
Jacksonville Beach, FL
D. Home: #36

KITCHEN DESIGN

CKD, Kitchen Studio1562
Kristi Wyndham, CKD
Jacksonville, FL
D. Home: #28

POOL DESIGN

SurfSide Pools
Jacksonville Beach, FL
D. Homes: #10, #44, #50 #63

Crystal Pools
D. Homes: #13, #61

Aqua Pool – Carolyn Sartor
D. Home: #18

Aquatic Consultants
Brian Van Bower
Miami, FL – D. Home: #23

Pools by John Clarkson
D. Homes: #31, #33

Landwise Design
Ladd Roberts
Jacksonville, FL
D. Home: #46

Overland Partners
Rick Archer, FAIA
San Antonio, TX
D.Home: #64

Parry Pools, Inc.
D. Home: #51

Florida Bonded Pools & James Dupree
D. Home: #52

MATERIAL SUPPLIERS

WINDOWS:

Anderson Windows
D. Homes: #3, #30, #37, #46, #47, #66

Tischler Und Sohn
D. Homes: #1, #12, #40

Zeluck, solid heart Honduran mahogany
D. Homes: #6, #57

Marvin Windows
D. Homes: #18, #21, #56

Pella Windows & French Doors
D. Homes: #6, #45

Fenestra Window & Door, Inc.
D. Homes: #23, #52

Luxbaum Impact
D. Home: #33

Pella Architectural Series - D. Home: #6

PGT Impact
D. Home: #43

HURD Impact Windows -
D. Home: #50

Weathershield Windows
D. Home: #63

Millwork & Doors:
Arte de Peru, Inc.
Gerald Buxbaum
D. Homes: #2, #13

FIREPLACES:

Isokern Masonry by Earthcore
D. Homes: #6, #37, #40, #46, #51, #61

ROOFING:

Monier Clay Tiles
D. Home: #45

BOOKS
DISTINCTIVE

For more information, recommendations for future *66 Distinctive Homes* books, other marketing opportunities or bulk purchasing, please contact Glenn Hettinger at:

WWW.66DISTINCTIVEHOMES.COM

TPC SAWGRASS
www.tpc.com/sawgrass

17TH ISLAND GREEN

All Photos Credit:
PGA TOUR/Photo Services

TPC Sawgrass — Home of THE PLAYERS Championship – encompasses more than 30 years of magic and memories from the famous pros' road to the Championship and everyday golfers who challenge THE PLAYERS Stadium Course and Dye's Valley Course. This Ponte Vedra Beach, FL landmark is open to the public and also offers annual pass programs for guests to experience golf and dining on a regular basis. The 77,000 square-foot Mediterranean Revival-style Clubhouse protects and shares the TPC Sawgrass history and heritage through THE PLAYERS memorabilia while golfers build new memories with storyteller forecaddies who help closely replicate the experiences of the pros. After world-class golf instruction and state-of-the-art equipment at the TOUR Academy that prepare links men for the 17th Island Green, one of the most challenging holes in the world, restaurants Nineteen and Traditions offer delectable dining and comfortable surroundings overlooking the famed fairways.

For more information on TPC Sawgrass please visit:
www.tpc.com/sawgrass

LXVI

SIXTY-SIX DISTINCTIVE HOMES

© Hettinger